Rick and Bubba's
Big Honkin'
Book of Grub

Rick and Bubba's
Big Honkin'
Book of Grub

By Rick Burgess and Bill "Bubba" Bussey

With Martha Bolton

THOMAS NELSON
Since 1798

NASHVILLE   DALLAS   MEXICO CITY   RIO DE JANEIRO

Published in Nashville, Tennessee, by Thomas Nelson. Thomas Nelson is a registered trademark of Thomas Nelson, Inc.

Published in association with the literary agency of Sanford Communications, Inc., now part of Credo Communications LLC, www.credocommunications.net

Thomas Nelson, Inc., titles may be purchased in bulk for educational, business, fund-raising, or sales promotional use. For information, please e-mail SpecialMarkets@ ThomasNelson.com.

"These are a few of my favorite things" (page 72) is borrowed from the song "My Favorite Things" from the 1959 Broadway musical *The Sound of Music*. Music by Richard Rodgers. Lyrics by Oscar Hammerstein II.

Library of Congress Cataloging-in-Publication Data

Burgess, Rick.
   Rick and Bubba's big honkin' book of grub / by Rick Burgess and Bill 'Bubba'
Bussey; with Martha Bolton.
     p. cm.
   ISBN 978-1-4016-0402-8
   1. Food—Humor. 2. American wit and humor. I. Bussey, Bubba. II. Bolton, Martha,
1951– III. Title.
   PN6231.F66B87 2010
   818'.602—dc22
                       2009048193

Printed in the United States of America

10 11 12 13 14 WRZ 5 4 3 2 1

This book is dedicated to all of you who at some time have put food on our plates:

Our moms

Our wives

Lunchroom ladies we've come to know and love throughout our lives

Each waiter and waitress who has ever served us

Each cook behind the scenes who made it happen

And each and every farmer who grows the food we love!

Contents

"All the fat is the Lord's . . ."

—Leviticus 3:16

The Rick and Bubba "Hey, You Gotta Live" Diet
^
non

Diet. Now, that's a word you hear every livelong day, *somewhere* in our carb-conscious society. Seems like every time I (Bubba) turn around, so-and-so's on a *diet*, or "Hey, man, what *diet* are you on?" or "Gee, she looks great. She must be *dieting*." If you ask us, there's a reason that the first three letters of the word *diet* are *d-i-e,*

Bubba begins another health food diet.

but hey, if YOU want to fuss with calories, points, or fat grams, we're with you.

Now, having offered you our support, if *you* want—or need—to go on a diet, there are a lot of different choices available to you today. You can do Atkins—if you're into that. Personally, we like our starch. God made it, and that's good enough for us. Or you could try Weight Watchers—if you dig counting all those little points for every sumptuous bite you put in your mouth . . . but Rick and I tend to cheat. (Individual chocolate chips don't *really* have points, do they? They're so small . . .) There's even the illustrious "Deal-a-Meal." (Ever notice how those old commercials make those ladies look like they're playing a fun game of cards? Hmph. I don't *think* so . . .) South Beach, North Beach, Sugar Busters, Weigh Down, count your calories, watch your zones, watch your this and watch your that— oh, the choices are endless. There's even a *caveman* diet. Hey, I could get into that! Anybody remember the size of that rack o' ribs Fred Flintstone was served in the closing credits of *The Flintstones*? Pass me the sauce!

But we are going to give you one *more* choice, *the*

quintessential diet. Introducing . . . (drum roll, please) the Rick and Bubba "Hey, You Gotta Live" diet. This is a diet plan that is based in reality, and it is what has kept us in *GQ* shape all these years.

The truth is, almost any diet will help you lose weight to some extent. That's because most diets are based on the simple principle that eating fewer calories than what you've been eating in the past will cause anyone to lose weight. It just makes mathematical sense.

But very few diets are set up for you to actually *live* while following them. Losing weight is fine, but if it's only to help you fit into your funeral clothes, what good is that? We contend that life is meant to be *lived*, and who can *live* without, say, carbs? (Hey, doctors tell us carbs have that "feel-good" thing going on for your brain. Who are we to argue?) A "diet" without mashed potatoes and French toast and Sister Schubert's yeast rolls and bottomless pasta bowls—we can't do it. And meat? Essential. Jesus ate meat. Who are we to tell him he's wrong? No sirree. *We* aren't about to go vegan.

No, with the Rick and Bubba "Hey, You Gotta Live"

diet plan, we don't discriminate against *any* particular type of food. In fact, with our diet, you can eat whatever you want.

Sugar? You got it!

White bread? Absolutely!

Animal fat? Here you go!

Red meat? Belly up to the carving table!

We're not so arrogant and narrow-minded as to leave out the very foods that everyone enjoys. That's not fair.

The funny thing is, this was two years before Don Juan even left. Any excuse for some cake.

Why should we punish butter? What did it do? Tasting good isn't a crime. At least the last time we checked it wasn't.

We're not going to single out desserts as the bad guy either. They're just trying to keep themselves in demand like everyone else—a little job security. Is that so bad?

Our philosophy is that we will continue to support *all* food. We say, eat *everything* . . . only do it in moderation. You can still go to buffets; just don't clean them out. And if you do, don't start licking the serving carts.

The Rick and Bubba "Hey, You Gotta Live" diet works on the truth principle. The truth is that people like us aren't fat because we're hungry. We're fat because we like how food tastes! That is a fact. We've faced it—now nutritionists need to face this truth too. They need to step back into reality. We love to eat. It's part of who we are.

I (Rick) don't order a hot fudge sundae because I'm starving. Nor do I order a second slice of cheesecake because I'm feeling weak and faint. If I were feeling weak and faint, I'd order a triple-meat burger or a sixteen-ounce steak or something a lot more filling and rich in iron. I order desserts because they don't care about iron. I order them because *they taste good*. I want that chocolate shake because I like the flavor of it, not because my stomach's growling

King Bubba having his cake and eating it too.

for it. (I haven't heard my stomach growl in fourteen years. I do my best to keep it full at all times. As its primary caregiver, I consider it my duty.)

So we say, why pretend that you don't want to eat? Of course you want to eat. You want more than the 1,800; 1,500; or 800 calories those other plans are limiting you to. Accept that truth. The goal of our diet isn't to get you to be skinny. Our goal is to get you to a level of fat that you can tolerate.

Having said all that, there *are* some folks out there—unlike Bubba and me—who really *do* eat because they're hungry—and only then. Our hats off to you. We'd like you better if you ate for fun, but hey, there's room for everybody on the Rick and Bubba "Hey, You Gotta Live" diet. For good, conscientious folks like you, there's only going to be one way for you to lose weight: stop eating when you're hungry, and instead, only eat when you're *famished*.

Now, many people confuse the terms *hungry* and *famished*, but there is a world of difference. Let Uncles Rick and Bubba help you.

First, *hungry* is a mild inconvenience. You may have

heard your stomach growl. The aroma coming from your kitchen may be making it difficult for you to concentrate on your favorite show. You may have even gotten a little faint. But this is not *famished*. It is *hungry*.

The way we look at it is this—*famished* is when you're hungry and nothing was done about it. This is far worse than being merely hungry. When you're famished, the waiter doesn't even have to ask if you want the pie, because you've already gone ahead and ordered it before you even ordered your meal.

Hungry means it's 11:30, and I'm a little spindly and lightheaded because it's almost lunchtime. *Famished* means it's 11:35, and it's time to get the IV going.

Hungry means I can be satisfied with one combo meal. *Famished* means I've moved beyond the *hungry* stage and am now combining combo meals. It means I'm coming off the menu board and I'm starting to make up my own combination numbers. *"I'll have three cheeseburgers, curly fries, and six tacos. Let's call that a #27."* Or I'll order one of the regular combo meals, and then start adding to it. *"I'll take a #4, plus two cheeseburgers and a side of beef."*

Hungry means I'm popping a frozen pizza into the oven. *Famished* means I'm eating it frozen . . . along with the box!

Hungry means my stomach is growling. *Famished* means *I* am.

Hungry means I've eaten all the chips and salsa and am now ready for my meal (but don't take away the chip bowl! Just keep fillin' 'er up, if you please . . .). *Famished* means I've eaten the centerpiece and half of the tablecloth, and I'm now in the kitchen, helping them cook.

Hungry means if the meat is not to my liking, I'll send it back to the chef. *Famished* means if the meat is still moving, I'm tackling it to the ground before it can get away.

So you see, for those of you—unlike Bubba and me—who don't eat because it's more fun than walking on a treadmill, more satisfying than a day at the zoo, and more a part of you than your own hair follicles, *your* success lies in your ability to distinguish between "Gee-that-smells-tasty-and-I-haven't-eaten-since-breakfast"—hungry—and "Unhand-that-pork-chop-or-I'll-fight-you-for-it"—FAMISHED.

Rick and Bubba's Weight Loss Tips

Tip #1: Before weighing yourself, always put the turkey down first.

Tip #2: Never put both feet on the scale.

Tip #3: Before weighing yourself, remove shoes, jewelry, and any dental fillings that may be adding to your weight.

Tip #4: Better yet, when the nurse isn't looking, "accidentally" fall against the scale, sliding the metal gauge down about ten pounds.

Tip #5: Buy bigger belts.

Tip #6: Only put three scoops of bacon bits on your salad.

Tip #7: Drop all your skinny friends. Only hang around people who are larger than you.

Tip #8: Jog, instead of walking, to your refrigerator.

Tip #9: All 31 flavors will not fit on a single ice cream cone. You have to choose. Deal with it.

Tip #10: Limit your intake of white flour. Wait until it's in a loaf of bread. It tastes better.

Rick and Bubba's "Get Out of Jail Free" Card

They say that, often, prisoners who finally get out of jail end up right back in the slammer—for the very same thing they got arrested for in the first place, or worse (at least that's what they say . . .). Well, it's our contention that most *dieters* are just like that.

Isn't it true that most other diet plans make you feel like you've been taken prisoner? And as a prisoner, sooner or later you're going to want to break out of your confinement of limited calories and make a run for it . . . to the nearest Krispy Kreme. So we ask you, what good was all that dieting you suffered through when you gain all that lost weight right back—and a couple or ten pounds more—before you're twenty feet beyond the drive-thru window?

It all seems like a waste to us. Who wants to step on a scale after a maple bar binge and see the same, pre-diet number that was there before the diet even began? It's defeating.

Was it worth passing on that wedding cake two weeks ago?

Was it worth waving off that banana pudding?

Was it worth sending the dessert cart on its way?

Of course it wasn't. If you're going to commit the same lip-lickin' crime as before and gain all your weight back, why bother going through all that dieting anguish in the first place? Get out of jail free, and enjoy the autonomy of the Rick and Bubba "Hey, You Gotta Live" diet plan.

Hey, Bubba, "autonomy"? That's kind of a fancy word for you.

Shhhh . . .

Another point we'd like to make about our diet plan is that we refuse to let you eat any strange versions of regular food. This includes fat-free chips of any kind. Chips were never intended to be fat free. They're deep-fried . . . in FAT. That's what makes them chips. Why pretend that you're eating something healthy when you've got a bag of Lay's in your hand? Oh, you can rationalize the part about it being a potato and having vitamins and all, but it's still a potato *chip*. Potato chips aren't a diet food. Quit pretending you can make them into a diet food.

Besides, have you read the side effects of fat-free chips? Read about them the next time you've got a bag of fat-free chips in your hand. Not one of those side effects is pretty. If you're going to diet, then just eat less food. Don't start messing around with "diet" versions of regular food that were never meant to be fat free.

Fat-free cheesecake? Fat-free ice cream? Fat-free butter? Fat-free *fat*? Haven't we carried this practical joke on long enough? To quote one of our favorite thin bodies, "Stop the insanity!"

> Er, Rick, I don't think that's what she meant.

> Shhh . . .

Besides, the fat-free marketers mess with your head anyway. Ever notice how labels on canned vegetables will sometimes brag about being "A Fat-Free Food"? Well, of *course* they're fat free. They're green beans—without butter. Or lard. Or those little fried-onion things that MeMaw puts on her green bean casserole. So you can't trust fat-free marketing. So why bother? Nutshell version? *Steer clear of fat-free foods.*

Rick says, "Yep. Plenty of fat in this stuff."

We also suggest that you stay away from diet drinks. It is our opinion that diet sodas are far worse for you than regular sodas. Artificial sweeteners are fine if you need them for health reasons; but if you don't, why would you risk putting chemicals you can't even pronounce in your body? The FDA may say they're perfectly fine, but we wonder about the safety of any chemical that can make your insides produce noises of a decibel level that NASA hasn't even heard yet.

Better yet, maybe we should all be drinking more water. And not pricey bottled water either. In this economy, do you have any idea how much money you could save by going back to drinking water out of the faucet? Remember that kind of water? It's still there. It may not have tiny little bubbles in it, but it's wet and costs a lot less. Besides, do you *really* believe that fancy-pants bottled stuff comes from "a sparkling Alpine stream"? Heck no, baby. It really comes from the murky waters of Swamp Holler—but who's gonna tell you *that*?

Aside from the freedom of eating what you want, when you want, another reason we feel the Rick and Bubba "Hey, You Gotta Live" diet plan has been so successful is the accompanying Rick and Bubba products, such as the Rick and Bubba governor for forks. This device works like any other governor device, only you attach it to your fork. The governor then sounds an alarm whenever your fork is exceeding the lift limit. Ignore it and severe penalties will apply, such as having all your fork privileges revoked. You won't be allowed to get behind the prongs of a fork until you have sought rehabilitation.

But the real secret behind the success of our diet plan has little to do with any of the above reasons. It is this: the return of the 8-inch plate. The average plate today will run about 12 inches. That size plate holds far too much food. We suggest returning to 8-inch plates, like our fore-fathers used, but then piling them as high as you can. Because of the size difference, and the clearance limit of most restaurants, you would naturally be eating less, yet it would look like so much more.

Make one small change like this and you could be well on your way to the weight of your dreams.

We also advocate a free day. You can call it a Day of Decadence, Day of Liberty, Day of Blowing Your Diet to Smithereens—whatever you want. This is the day when you can eat as much as you want without any guilt whatsoever, but only on this one day. We feel that by providing this kind of freedom to our dieters, by allowing them to let loose on this one day each week, they will find it easier to keep to their diet on the other six days. We've tested this out ourselves, and it really does seem to have a positive effect on a dieter's mental state.

That's right, by having two freedom days per week, we are more likely to maintain our diet regimen for the other five days. Let's face it, diets are hard to maintain, but we have found that by allowing ourselves these three freedom days each week, we are able to pass on unhealthy snacks and desserts the other four days of the week. Four freedom days aren't really that many when you get right down to it.

Imagine it—five days in which you can eat anything you like, and only two during which you have to watch your caloric intake. That sounds reasonable, doesn't it? Six free days, and only one diet day. Tell us a diet plan that is easier than that. Seven free days, and zero diet days.

That's the Rick and Bubba diet. *Sign up today!*

The Incredible,
Edible . . . Meat?

Rick and I (Bubba) are reminded of the inspiring Bible story of Jesus, after he'd been away from his disciples for a while, and he asks them, "Do you have any *meat*?" (Trust us: it's in there.) Notice he didn't say, "Do you have any *rice cakes*?" or "Do you have any *fat-free alfalfa sprouts*?" No sir. The Man wanted *meat*. Now, at the risk of repeating ourselves, Rick and I would just like to say, in all humility and deference—

> Bubba, dude, those are AWFULLY *big* words.

> SHHHH!

—that if it's good enough for our Lord, it's good enough for us. We're contentedly carnivorous. But we've already talked about Jesus being a meat-eater and all, so far be it from us to belabor the point. What's important now is that you understand that meat is your friend. The cavemen ate it. Hey, they didn't discover fire for nothing! What do you *think* they did that for? Well, we can tell you. Ol' Neanderthal (or whoever he was) came up with the idea of fire for . . .

The World's First Barbeque

Now, really. Wouldn't you like to meet the first person to try milk? Who looked at a cow's udder and said, "You know what? I think I'm going to get me a cup of that!" Who had that kind of courage?

We don't think it just happened. We believe that some guy was milking a cow and got a little of the milk on his hands. Then, when he went to wipe the sweat off his face, he accidentally got some of the creamy substance on his lips, took a taste, and said, "Hey, that's not so bad."

Learning to milk a cow and drink what it was giving had to have been a process. But a lot of food developed like that. Someone tried it out first, and then, if it was good and they didn't die, they told their friends and neighbors about it.

And that, my friends, is precisely what happened with barbeque. Everyone was huddled around the camp one night, and it was freezing cold, and they invented fire. (Hey, don't ask for details. We don't know how they did it. We weren't there.) Then someone said, "Whoa! That feels good! That feels *real* good—but I'm hungry as a bear!"

Then someone grunted, "Hey, let's throw that woolly mammoth on those flames and see what happens." So they did. You know they had to have liked that mammoth rump a lot better than what they had been eating up to that point.

But then, we all know what followed next. Someone said, "It's good, but it's a little bland. Why don't we try a little seasoning?" So they squashed some juice out of this and mixed it with a few of the seeds from that and mashed it all together and—eureka! They found it. Barbeque sauce. And for the first time ever, they munched on woolly mammoth à la Heinz 57. And the rest, as they say, is history.

Then along came . . .

TURKEY!

Now, we'll talk more about turkey later, because there's a whole list of do's and don'ts governing the proper eating of certain parts of a turkey, but in the meantime, can you imagine what that first Thanksgiving meal was like? The Pilgrims and Indians probably sat down to barbequed turkey, and it wasn't long before one Indian said, "You know what? I think I prefer the vinegar-base barbeque sauce."

Then a Pilgrim said, "What? Are you outta your mind! Tomato base is best!"

No doubt the two continued to argue over which sauce was best until they finally were sitting at opposite ends of the table. (Of course, *we* know which sauce is best. That's why we're giving you the recipe *for free* in our secret recipe file.)

The tensions might have even escalated to the topic of which side made the best ribs.

It probably never got resolved peacefully (these kinds of arguments never do), which may or may not have led up to the final battle between them.

Who's to say? But it could've happened that way.

Top Ten Reasons Why the Turkey Toss Should Be an Olympic Event

10. To confuse all the other countries.

9. To honor Ben Franklin, who always wanted the turkey to be the national bird.

8. It's more exciting to watch than curling. (Come on, admit it! You know it's true.)

7. Who wouldn't love to see the Chinese teams do it?

6. As soon as the event is over, one word—dinnertime!

5. It's the perfect punishment for the Olympic committee for removing girls softball (as a coach and supporter of girls softball, we think it deserves to be in the Olympics!).

4. It gives Bubba hope for winning Olympic gold.

3. To ignite fans to start chanting, "Where's the dressing?"

2. To cut out the middleman when trying to give food to Third World countries. As soon as the turkey lands, it's just, "Here, take some!"

1. Because it would be appointment television. You know it would.

And speaking of ribs, we *love* . . .

PORK: THE "OTHER" WHITE MEAT!

Now, we all know that pork gets a bad rap. Has for a long time, and we can't help that. But then one day, some ingenious guy from—who knows?—the National Association of Folks Who Love Pork Chops came up with a slogan that is celebrated by pig lovers everywhere: "Pork: The Other White Meat ®." Hey, some pork *is* white (if you scrape off all that barbeque sauce), and we all know that white meat is good for you, so there you go.

So now, having redeemed the reputation of our pot-bellied pals, we'd like to offer a long-overdue tribute to another porkified food that needs no long introduction. Ladies and gentlemen, we present to you:

BACON!

Now, we realize that some of our readers may have a religious conviction about eating pork, and by no means do we want to cause anyone to stumble. But as for ourselves, being Gentiles and all, we have again embraced the words of Jesus when he said that (and we are paraphrasing here) what comes out of our mouths is a greater problem than what goes into our mouths.

In other words, this could be what he meant:

Gossip? Problem.

Bacon? Not so much.

Bearing false witness? Problem.

Bacon? Have at it.

Backstabbing a friend? Problem.

Bacon? Enjoy.

Blasphemy? Big problem.

Bacon? A burger couldn't find a better partner.

Jesus' words could possibly be interpreted to mean: "If people would spend half the time thinking about the words they say, instead of what they were going to eat, the world would be a much better place."

So, maybe bacon got a reprieve. Lucky for us, because we love those little strips of fatty meat.

That said, we encourage everyone reading this book to go back to those days of sleeping late on a Saturday morning and waking up to the outstanding aroma of bacon frying in a pan. Trust us: it'll make a smile spread across your face. See, you're smiling right now, aren't you? That smell is so wonderful and strong, you can even smell it in a daydream. For the life of us, we can't figure out why it's not a perfume already. What man could possibly be upset with a wife or girlfriend who smelled like bacon? What husband wouldn't follow his bride to the ends of the earth if she dabbed a little hickory-smoked pig fat behind her ears?

There's something about bacon that makes any meal better. Just look what it can do to a simple sandwich or hamburger. When bacon comes to a plate, a celebration breaks out. When we crunch it up into tiny bits and put it on some lettuce leaves, suddenly a dull, meaningless salad becomes something a man can even eat in front of other men.

Bacon, you are so simple and yet so wonderful. We salute you! We humbly thank you for all you have done to improve our breakfasts, lunches, and dinners. We will be forever in your debt.

For all you do, bacon, we do hereby declare October 7 as the official Rick and Bubba's National Bacon Day.

But, you know . . . bacon strips aren't the only bites of bliss that can be gleaned from the scrumptious and savory swine. There's also . . .

SAUSAGE!

Like many of us who have gone through life not knowing what we're made of, so it is with sausage. Sausage has been called "mystery meat," and other terms of non-endearment, but through it all, sausage has held its head high. It has stood proud, right there next to bacon and ham in most grocery stores, and it has never once cowered in the corner in shame.

Pig lips or pig snouts? Who knows and who cares! It's just so *tasty*! It is for this reason that we honor sausage today and hereby make the following proclamation:

Whereas sausage has never once acted like a second-class meat, but has always and faithfully answered the call to sizzle.

Whereas sausage has had the boldness to be honest in its listing of ingredients simply by using these five simple words: "Yes, it's probably in here."

Whereas sausage, even with an occasional complaint of a bone in its mix, or some other foreign product that could easily chip a tooth, will not allow itself to be deterred from duty.

Whereas all of the above has been found to be true, we do hereby declare May 1 Rick and Bubba National Sausage Day.

Enjoy!

Now, let's move on to another cut of meat. And folks, this one's critical. You see, something tragic has been going on in our society unchecked. We've seen it done on television sitcoms, at various school cafeterias across the nation, around dinner tables in otherwise peaceful homes, and at a good percentage of the campgrounds in America. What is it? *The open and vocal disrespect of . . .*

SPAM!

We're usually not this politically correct, but enough is enough. Someone has to stand up for this too-often-maligned meat product. Spam has been dissed for long enough, and it's time someone defended this faithful can of gelled meat.

Spam has been showing up on sandwiches and dinner plates ever since 1937. We even went to the Spam festival one year and saw it used in cake and ice cream recipes. Spam is nothing if not versatile.

But even as well-meaning as most of these festival entries were, did the contestants realize what they were doing? Were they shaming Spam into being something it isn't? Spam can't help that it's not sold in the meat section of the grocery store. We're sure it wanted to be, but that's not where most store managers stock it. It's usually over by the tuna and canned chicken. Isn't that already enough humiliation? Do people have to take it one step further and toss it into cake batter or churn it into a frozen dessert?

Don't get us wrong. We're not saying that these Spam festivals don't pay due homage to the King of Canned Meats. They do. We're just saying that Spam cake and Spam ice cream may be a little over-the-top. Spam has a hard enough time being accepted as a meat, and this sort of thing can't be helping it any.

While we're at it, we'd like to ask you restaurant owners and managers a question. How come we never see Spam on your menus? A tuna sandwich will be there. Even a tuna melt. We can easily find a chicken sandwich made from canned chicken. We've seen fried bologna sandwiches. But who among you is offering a Spam sandwich? We've yet to see one of those listed, even though people happily eat them at home all the time. You've probably eaten your share of them too. So isn't this a bit hypocritical? It's like we're all pretending that we don't eat Spam, which we know clearly isn't the case. Are we ashamed of this little can of meat?

Where's our loyalty, folks? And after all that Spam has done for us over the years, too. When we were out of fresh meat, it came to our rescue and gladly filled in. When we were all out of bacon and sausage, but needed something else to go with our eggs and toast, it stepped up to the skillet.

And yet, when it comes to dining out, we pretend like we've never even heard of this canned meat product. Like we're above ordering it in public. Even at the grocery store we look around before reaching for it, and then, once we do pick it up, we tuck it under the rest of our groceries in the cart just in case we run into the neighbors and they'll think we can't afford better cuts of meat.

We're pathetic.

But just so that all the world will know that Spam is valuable indeed, may we present . . .

Spam 'n' Taters

Ingredients:

3	pounds potatoes, cubed
2	cans Spam
6	tablespoons butter, plus extra butter for greasing the casserole dish
3	tablespoons flour
1½	cups milk
1	(8-ounce) bag shredded cheddar cheese

Directions:

- Boil the potatoes and drain. Set aside.

- Cube the Spam.

- Grease a 2-quart casserole dish with butter. Layer the potatoes and Spam (two layers of each) in the casserole dish. Set aside.

- Melt the 6 tablespoons of butter in a saucepan. Stir in the flour until brown and bubbly. Add the milk, stirring constantly until the mixture thickens. Blend in the cheese until melted. Pour over the Spam and potatoes, and warm in the microwave or oven. Serve.

Top Ten Reasons to Attend
the Annual Spam Festival

10. Spam is one of the few foods left that is 100 percent recession-proof.

9. Spam is the undefeated processed meat of the new millennium.

8. How else can you find out how to make Spam pudding?

7. Ever seen the Empire State Building made completely out of Spam?

6. To see a live production of *Spamalot* done by local actors.

5. To see the Spam version of *Gone with the Wind*, where Rhett Butler says that famous line, "Frankly, Scarlett, I don't give a Spam!"

4. To see if anyone can finally answer the question, "What is Spam?"

3. For tips on how to grill Spam and to keep it from falling into the fire.

2. To see if that weird gel stuff that covers the meat is really some kind of adhesive.

1. Because the family that eats Spam together stays together.

And what about this persecuted cut of beef (or chicken, or pork, or . . .):

THE HOT DOG!

The egg may be incredible. Honey may be a virtual fountain of youth. But we admire the hot dog. The hot dog is an unapologetic food. It doesn't have to tell you what all is inside of it. It figures beef, pork, chicken, or turkey is all the information you need to go on. It can lie there on its bun and dare you to take a bite of it. It's a proud food. It is, in fact, the *perfect food*.

We're a little baffled, then, as to why it feels it has to use so many aliases. Think about it. The hot dog has been called frankfurter (frank for short), weenie, wiener, and dog. But even with this odd, somewhat paranoid behavior, we still admire it. What other food would wrap itself in intestine lining and dare to show up on the dining table? Other foods know they would be laughed out of the room. The hot dog doesn't care.

The hot dog knows who it is. It knows you either like it or you don't. It doesn't bother it either way. It's so confident, it doesn't mind being served with only beans. Or sauerkraut. Give it a bottle of ketchup and it's a meal.

The hot dog doesn't make excuses for itself, and it doesn't cower to anybody.

There are some people in life that you wish you could have met. We wish we could have met the inventor of indoor plumbing, the creator of air-conditioning, and the guy who first decided to put all the leftover animal parts together, shove it into that intestine lining, twist it into a sausage shape, and then stand back and say, "Hey, let's try this."

We are eternally grateful for that kind of courage.

Now, pass the relish.

The Bun/Hot Dog Treaty of 2010

We the undersigned do hereby publicly apologize to the American public for the practical joke we have played on everyone for decades now.

We the undersigned fully admit before God and all those reading this today that we knowingly shorted our hot dog bun packages by two buns. We did, in fact, fully realize that hot dogs came in packages of ten, but we thought it would be funny to put only eight hot dog buns in our packages.

Apparently, it was not.

We the undersigned wish for the public to understand that this was simply a little food industry humor (like when the makers of Oreos "accidentally" made their cookies "inside out." You thought that was funny, didn't you?).

Regardless, we have realized—some may say too late—that you didn't see the humor in our little joke. We actually realized it shortly after we first did it, but by then we had already shipped hundreds of thousands of eight-bun packages, and contracted for millions more. We were in too deep to gracefully get out of it.

We tried to get the hot dog industry to reduce the number of weenies in their packages by two, but they have always refused to adjust their number of hot dogs to cover our misjudgment.

As you know, the matter has also been taken up in courts all across this great land, with countless appeals, mistrials, and hung juries. Because of this, we no longer wish to go the litigation route. It is time-consuming and costly, and no one wins but the attorneys.

This is why we have met privately with the hot dog industry to negotiate a peaceful resolution to these long-standing differences. We are happy to say that the Bun/Hot Dog Treaty of 2010 is now a reality. We have come up with what we believe is a workable treaty between us.

The time has come for us to put an end to all this packaging madness. We no longer wish to be the butt of jokes by late-night comedians with their own talk shows, or to be a reference in humorous articles and sitcom dialogue.

Today, we, the hot dog bun industry, do hereby publicly

apologize for a joke that has gone on for far too long. We solemnly swear to cease this senseless confusion that has befuddled the public ever since the packaging was first introduced.

The hot dog industry, in like manner, does hereby agree to cease lording our bad joke over us.

We will now take the higher ground and begin adding two more buns to each of our packages. This change in policy will take effect immediately.

Of course, should the hot dog manufacturers pump up the number of hot dogs in a package to twelve, then we would then have to follow suit. If they drop down to six, then we would have to drop down to six. In spite of our desire to rectify the situation, this whole crazy game could continue for years.

On second thought, maybe we'll just leave well enough alone.

And who can we forget . . .

GIBLETS!

Yes, you heard me. Giblets. Now, some folks question whether giblets are, as they say in the sticks, "fittin'" to eat. Well, we know they are. First off, my (Rick's) Webster's dictionary says that giblets are "the edible viscera of a fowl." Now, I can't tell you what "viscera" is, but the word *edible* definitely caught my eye. And just so you'll know, *giblets* include that luscious liver, the delectable heart, the—well, the gizzard *might* not be so great; I guess it is if you like shoe leather—but anyway, the gizzard, and most times, the neck—which is also pretty worthless . . . Point is, don't consign the giblets to Fido's bowl (except maybe the gizzard and the neck)—or to your pan of dressing or giblet gravy. Eat that turkey liver yourself from time to time. It is a treat indeed.

And while we're talking about the merits of that little sack of giblets that comes inside of every whole chicken and turkey, there is an issue that is particularly troubling to Bubba and me . . .

YOU SAY JIBLET, I SAY GIBLET

We hate to keep bringing up controversial topics, but we can't write a book about food and not weigh in on the giblet versus jiblet debate.

The word is *giblet*. End of discussion.

But just so we don't get any letters, we'll go ahead and give you our reasons for coming to this conclusion.

First, you don't say, "Have you seen that pretty jirl," or "King Kong is a jorilla," do you? Of course not. The "g" has a "guh" sound, right?

We can hear you "jiblet people" coming back with, "Yeah, well, then, why don't we say 'Gorge' for George, instead of giving it a "j" sound as in 'Jeffrey'?"

All right. That's a valid point.

We don't want to quibble, but the problem as we see it is we have a letter that doesn't know how to act. It can't make up its mind which sound it wants to make. So we have to go to other sources to determine the correct pronunciation.

The authority that I (Rick) choose to go by on this matter is my memaw. My memaw was one of the godliest women I know, and I have to say that I never once heard her pray to "Jod." It was always to "God." My memaw had the backbone to keep the letter "g" in its place.

Another authority on this subject is Big Bird from *Sesame Street*. I remember one holiday episode when Big Bird was sleeping outside in the cold. The script called for him to say a line that I'll never forget as long as I live. Big Bird said that he was so cold, "his giblets were freezing." And he pronounced it with a "guh" sound.

It doesn't get any more authoritative than that, folks.

Both Big Bird and my memaw have convinced me beyond any reasonable doubt that it is *giblets*, not *jiblets*. Oh, and don't bother looking for "jiblets" in Webster's dictionary, either. It's not in there. Call them jiblets, if you must, but they *are* giblets. And I'm not going to waste any more time talking about it.

But I digress.

Now, for our final meat of the chapter . . .

SUSHI!

One thing that I (Bubba) have learned in life is to *never* say *never*. I used to make fun of people who ate sushi. I was merciless. I would accuse them of eating fish bait. I couldn't understand why anyone in the world would eat raw fish when they could fry it. It didn't make any sense to me.

But then my passion for tennis led me to another way of thinking.

The tennis was Betty's idea. The cake was Bubba's.

If you know me at all, then you know that I've always been a slave to physical fitness. My determination to maintain my lean and trim physique is what led me to take up the sport of tennis. And it is tennis that led me into the world of sushi. Let me explain.

One day while watching tennis on television, I heard several of the players discussing their love for sushi. They pointed out how sushi is a good source of protein and that it's low in fat. I have always been open to learning from other tennis players, so I allowed my love of tennis to overcome my fear of sushi, and I decided to give it a try.

Now, I should warn you—when you take those first steps down the sushi path, you can't simply go off on your own and start ordering everything off the sushi menu. You need a "sushi guide." Luckily, I found a gentleman who was willing to teach me "all things sushi."

He suggested I start slowly. He had me order the California roll and the volcano roll. Those weren't too bad. They were really quite tasty, in fact; so we moved on down the menu to the raw fish section. I tried salmon first, and then tuna and squid. To my surprise, I liked them. Since there were no trips to the emergency room yet, we moved a little further down the menu.

Sea bass and yellowtail came next, and I was doing great—so good that I figured I needed to be challenged in this new world. So I ordered sea eel and baby octopus. I'll be honest with you, octopus isn't my favorite, but it is fun to order and terrorize the other people at your table.

Eating sushi has made me feel a certain kinship with grizzly bears. I realize that we eat salmon the very same way. A grizzly bear will just reach into a cold stream and pull out a fish and start chomping down on it. That's kind of what I'm doing when I eat sushi. So, in a way, I guess you could say that bears are sushi eaters. (Oh, yeah, and Jesus ate fish . . .)

Another thing I like about sushi is how easy it is to chew. There's hardly any work involved. You just put it in your mouth and chomp down a few times, and it's gone. It's not like a tough steak or stringy asparagus.

What I don't understand about sushi, though, is why it takes so long to get my order. It's *raw* fish. There's no cooking involved! What takes them so long, then, to make it? I'll have dinner guests with me, and their cooked order will arrive at our table before my raw fish does. Does this make sense to anyone?

Some of my friends have warned me that I should be concerned about the possible mercury content of raw fish. But I've looked into this issue myself. I called the health department, but the worker, who shall remain nameless, said that there are fewer reports of food poisoning from sushi than from salad bars.

Today, I consider myself a sushi connoisseur. I have conquered my fear and preconceived prejudice against this food product. I eat sushi at least two or three times a week for lunch, and I am able to order anything on the menu. I feel better, I'm leaner, and for some reason I love to rub up and down against a tree to scratch my back.

But I'm sure that's temporary.

So, there you have it. Meat's good for you, the Lord ate it, and we like it. So, in the words of our good ol' fellow Alabamian, Forrest Gump, "That's all I have to say about that."

Other Foods
We Like

"Man shall not live by meat alone . . ."

No sir, we are *not* poking fun at the Good Book. Rick and I (Bubba) are the Bible's biggest fans. And yes, we know the verse really says *bread*, not *meat*. We're simply trying to make a point: though we love our meat—and in every variety—just like bread, by itself, *it ain't enough*!

To get the full effect out of whatever roadkill's on your plate, you've gotta have the other stuff—and that's what this chapter's about: other foods we like. Let's start with . . . *casserole*!

Rick and Bubba's Tribute to the Casserole

What can we say about the casserole that hasn't already been written in ER medical reports all across this great land of ours?

Over the years the casserole has become a mainstay of the American diet, and it's easy to see why: virtually no preparation. Or recipe. You just toss in whatever you have sitting around in your refrigerator (including some of that roadkill mentioned above)—preferably within a month or two of its expiration date—toss in some noodles, and voilà—instant dinner.

Can any of us imagine life without the casserole? There would be no more church potlucks, no more sports team picnics, and no more post-funeral gatherings. Social life as we know it today would drastically change. That's because the casserole has become a fundamental part of society. And now, with this current economic situation, many families are turning to the casserole for their very survival.

Yes, we owe a lot to this scoopable, all-in-one meal. It has given us something to put in our mega-baking dishes that haven't seen the inside of an oven in decades. It has fed our families, our neighbors, our friends, and even people we didn't much care for. It has been our salvation between paychecks, and our lunches for weeks after the original casserole appeared on our table.

The only negative we see with the casserole is that many, if not all, of them look exactly alike. A tuna casserole is almost impossible to tell apart from a turkey casserole, and a cheddar sausage casserole is equally difficult to tell apart from a cheesy chili mac casserole. You never know which one you're eating until you taste it, and even then, you could be wrong. You could be eating out of the dog dish by mistake.

Do you realize that if, years ago, someone hadn't run low on food, the casserole might never have been invented? If some poor guy hadn't returned home from his hunting trip empty-handed again, causing his wife to have to improvise with whatever leftovers they had, we wouldn't have the casserole today.

The casserole has become our mother, our Aunt Bee, our Marie Callender, bringing us comfort on cold nights and in hard times. It has seen us through our years of want, and has become so much a part of us that we'll gladly eat it even when there are other options.

For this reason, we pause today to pay homage to this great family dish.

Casserole—we salute you! You have served us well. For your years of service, going above and beyond the call of duty, we do hereby declare June 13 Rick and Bubba's National Casserole Day.

RICK AND BUBBA'S
BEEFY CHEESE CASSEROLE

Ingredients:

1/2   pound ground beef

1   tablespoon butter, melted

3   tablespoons minced onion

1   (8-ounce) can tomato sauce

1/2   teaspoon salt

    Dash of pepper

1/2   cup sour cream

1/2   cup cream-style cottage cheese

3   tablespoons chopped parsley

1/2   cup sliced, cooked carrots

4   ounces noodles, cooked and drained

    Grated cheese, for topping

Directions:

- Preset the oven to 350 degrees.

- Brown the ground beef in melted butter; add the onion and sauté until the onion is transparent. Stir in the tomato sauce, salt, and pepper; simmer, uncovered, for 5 minutes or until thickened. Set aside.

- In a bowl, combine the sour cream, cottage cheese, parsley, and carrots; gently stir in the cooked noodles. In a greased baking dish, layer half of the meat mixture, half of the cottage cheese mixture, and the remaining meat mixture, and finish with the cottage cheese mixture. Top with grated cheese and bake for 25 to 30 minutes, or until bubbly.

Dressing: It's in There!

Now that you're thoroughly convinced that casseroles are God's gift to the working world, let's talk about another food that no food lover should live a day or two without: dressing—and I'm (Rick) not talking about Thousand Island.

Dressing is one of the most incredible foods ever invented. Sad to say, there are folks in some parts of this great country who have not yet experienced the thrill of eating dressing. My heart breaks for them. All American citizens have the right to dressing, as outlined in our Constitution (I'm sure it's in there). So why these individuals would deny themselves this inalienable right is beyond me.

Maybe it's because dressing has become what is known today as a "recreational food." We only eat it on special occasions, and then, we forget all about it the rest of the year.

Dressing deserves so much more.

Mashed potatoes don't get treated like this. They can be served at any meal throughout the year. You can have mashed potatoes every night for dinner if you so choose. You can have them for lunch. I suppose you could even have them for breakfast, as some people do at all-you-can-eat brunches. As far as I know, there is no restriction limiting the consumption of mashed potatoes.

But I have never once called my wife, or even my mom when we're having dinner at her house, and asked what was on the menu, and heard the word "dressing" mentioned, unless it was one of the big two holidays—Christmas or Thanksgiving.

Doesn't this seem a little small-minded to you?

It isn't dressing's fault. Where can you find ready-made dressing just any old time of the year? During the holidays, maybe. But doubtful, even then.

And look in your cookbooks, ladies. Where are all the good (and bad) dressing recipes? Uh-huh, in the holiday section. With turkey.

And even that horrible stuff that comes in a box and

is passed off as dressing (but it's *not*; it's *stuffing*, and we hate it!) can only be found in a bin in the middle of a grocery store aisle—not on the shelves—in November and December. Any other time of year, it's nowhere to be found (not that we care—that "stuff's" not dressing!).

That's why I'm stepping forward today to address the dressing dilemma once and for all. I say the medical world should issue a public advisory that recommends eating dressing at least three times a week, like they do for fish. Has anyone looked into the healthful benefits of a scoop of dressing? If the recipe includes cream of chicken soup, chicken broth, chicken or turkey parts, onions, and herbs, there must be some health benefits.

So why are we saving this possible miracle food for only two holidays, and relegating it mostly to the inside of a turkey carcass? Why not have Easter dressing, slapped between thick slices of country ham? Or a Fourth of July menu of hot dogs and dressing? Better yet, why not serve it on ordinary nights, like say, Thursday? Or obscure Tuesday? Is there anything wrong with these days seeing a little dressing?

While discussing dressing on the radio once, a listener called in to ask us if either one of us had ever personally made dressing. We confessed that we hadn't. She said if we had, we'd know why we only get it twice a year.

Apparently, dressing isn't all that easy to make. We were not aware of this. So we checked with our wives. They confirmed this.

Case in point . . .

Homemade Cornbread Dressing

Ingredients:

FOR THE CORNBREAD

2½	cups white, self-rising cornmeal
2	cups whole milk
4	cups water
6	tablespoons butter
1¼	cups sugar
2	teaspoons salt
3	eggs, beaten

FOR THE DRESSING

6	cups crumbled cornbread
2	cups bread crumbs
2	tablespoons flour dissolved in 1 cup water
2	cups chopped celery
2	cups chopped onions
4	eggs, beaten
1	stick butter, melted
2	cans cream of chicken soup (optional)
	Salt and pepper to taste
	Chicken or turkey stock

Directions:

- The day before you intend to make the dressing, bake the cornbread as follows:

- Preheat the oven to 450 degrees.

- In a large mixing bowl, mix together the cornmeal and the milk. Set aside.

- In a large saucepan, heat the water and butter just to the boiling point. Add the sugar, salt, and beaten eggs. Add the cornmeal mixture and cook, stirring constantly, until the mixture boils and is very thick. Be careful not to scorch.
- Pour the cornbread mixture into a greased baking pan and bake in the oven until light brown on top (no more than 20 minutes).
- The next day, make the dressing:
- Preheat the oven to 400 degrees.
- Crumble the cornbread.
- In a very large bowl, sift together the cornbread crumbs and the white breadcrumbs. Add the flour and water mixture, the celery, the onions, the eggs, the butter, and the soup. Stir until moistened. Salt and pepper to taste.
- Add the poultry stock until the mixture is soupy in consistency. Bake in the oven until the dressing is golden brown and thick enough to scoop.

Stuffing, on the other hand, seems much simpler: just open the box, follow the directions—and immediately *give to the cat*.

Which leads me to a topic of grave concern to Bubba and me:

The Great "Dressing vs. Stuffing" Debate

Okay, okay, I know this is a nation where *tolerance* rules the day, but come on. Some things are just nonnegotiable. *Dressing* is a gift from the heavens. *Stuffing*? Um, wouldn't wanna eat it. And we don't care where you're from, New York or Sacramento, Seattle or Miami, *stuffing* is for the birds—and not the kind of bird you eat. (Oh, wait. We just said to feed it to the cat . . .)

As we already said, Bubba and I have learned our lesson: *dressing* is hard to make. Takes time. Blood. Sweat. Tears too, when you're chopping those onions. But stuffing? Well, really, how hard is it to dampen some old croutons and then heat them up? That's all stuffing is, isn't it? Soggy croutons? At least that's what it looks like when you open the box.

Isn't that why they call it stuffing? Because it's just *stuff*?

Whatever is in it, one thing's for sure—dressing is better. Bubba and I have had plenty of stuffing in our lifetimes. We know stuffing. And believe us, stuffing is no dressing.

Dressing is like that brother you could never live up to and always had to stay behind, walking in his shadow. In the food family, stuffing is the lesser brother. It's like an afterthought that the bird had. Like the bird felt sorry for you because you didn't have any real dressing, so he said, "Okay, here's a little something I left behind for you."

No wonder stuffing has a complex. It knows it can never live up to dressing. We feel bad for it, but truth is truth.

I understand that stuffing was first discovered when someone gathered all the scraps off the plates and put it into a pile on a used serving tray. Someone arrived late to the dinner and unknowingly said, "Here, let me have a bite of that."

The rest is stuffing history.

It is our opinion, then, that the only time you should eat stuffing is when dressing is not available. Stuffing is what taxidermists talk about. It is not a food. *Dressing* is a food. Stuffing's what's inside your pillow. *Dressing* goes . . .

Over the lips, between the gums
Look out, stomach! Here it comes!

Now that I've explained the differences between stuffing and dressing, and testified to the superiority of dressing, I would like to address the different kinds of dressing.

I prefer my dressing either so thick that you cut it into squares, or more like a casserole where you scoop it out of the dish. These are my favorites, and I stick to them.

Bubba has ventured into some of these new shapes of dressing. He once shared a Thanksgiving meal with some friends in Kentucky, and they served their dressing in balls. I'm not so sure about this. How do you know how many balls it takes to be the equivalent of two scoops of dressing? I don't want to have to make a decision like that and end up underestimating the number of balls required for a normal serving of dressing. I don't want to take a ball and a half when I should be taking three balls. Who needs that kind of stress? Family gatherings have enough pressure without adding dressing-ball issues.

Another thing I would like to bring up is something I've accepted for years, but have really been bothered about. Why are people putting *chicken* meat in their dressing? I can handle chicken broth, and even the cream of chicken soup. But using chicken meat in a turkey dressing seems a little deceptive. And pushy. It's turkey's day. Why is the chicken pushing its way in?

Everyone knows that when you cook a turkey, there will be extra turkey meat in the giblets and other pieces of turkey in that bag they hide inside the bird. So why aren't more people using this turkey meat in the dressing? Why are they cooking a separate chicken just to use in the dressing? How did a chicken get in on the party? I understand the whole principle of two birds being better than one, but this doesn't seem fair to the bigger bird. The poor turkey barely gets two days out of the year; but now, here comes the chicken horning in on his turf. It's not right, and we're not going to stand for it anymore. Someone has to stand up and make their voice heard in defense of the turkey.

It's the turkey's day! Most of us already eat chicken three or four times a week . . . if not more. Poor ol' Tom gets a couple of days and that's it. Can't the chicken quit being a hog and back off so the turkey can get some long overdue attention?

It's only right.

So . . . what were we talking about, anyway? Oh yeah: other foods we like. Which immediately brings to mind . . .

Rick and Bubba's Two Most Underrated Foods

Peanut Butter

Peanut butter may be a simple food, but life doesn't get any better than when you've got a jar of creamy peanut butter in your lap, along with a box of Ritz crackers. Now, I (Rick) don't want to get on my soapbox about crunchy versus creamy. My wife happens to be a crunchy, while I, on the other hand, am a creamy, through and through. At one time I almost had everyone in our house sold on creamy, but then my wife, Sherri, said something about being a grown woman and able to make her own decisions. The next thing I know, peanut butter confusion was back in our home.

I'm sorry, but there's just something weird about crunchy peanut butter. It's like someone started eating some peanuts, but didn't finish and spit them out. It's not a pretty visual, but it's close to accurate, am I right? Crunchy peanut butter doesn't feel natural in my mouth. It also tends to break the crackers in half. And if you bite down on a mouthful of crunchy peanut butter the wrong way, it can break a tooth.

On the other hand, creamy peanut butter sits perfectly smooth atop a cracker, and it goes down smooth, too. No need for dental work here. It simply serves its purpose and it goes on its way.

Frankly, there is no better snack.

Now, I don't want to unfairly influence anyone, but if you're going to serve peanut butter, it should be Jif. Choosy moms choose Jif. So do choosy and sexy fat people. At least these two do.

Ah, peanut butter . . . the almost nearly perfect food.

Since we've taken the time to convince you that peanut butter deserves its place in every kitchen, allow us to offer you a yummy way to use your jar of Jif:

RICK AND BUBBA'S PEANUT BUTTER BARS OF JOY

Ingredients:

4	large graham crackers
1/2	cup butter
1	cup peanut butter
1/2	pound powdered sugar
1	large chocolate bar

Directions:

- Put graham crackers in a plastic bag or between sheets of waxed paper; crush with a rolling pin or hammer. (Graham crackers can also be crushed in a blender.) Set aside. In a large saucepan, slowly melt the butter over low heat. Remove from heat. Blend in the crushed graham crackers, peanut butter, and powdered sugar until completely mixed. Press into an 8-inch square pan. In the top of a double boiler, melt the chocolate bar; spread on the peanut butter mixture. Let cool and cut into bars.

Hush Puppies

One of the most underappreciated foods in the world is the hush puppy. These little balls of deep-fried joy, these golden nuggets of goodness, these spheres of deep-fried ecstasy are often all but ignored on a dinner plate.

So we ask you—why has the hush puppy not been properly embraced?

We feel the hush puppy has been overlooked because it is small, and okay, at times it can be a bit greasy. But so are a lot of other foods, and they don't get ignored on the plate as if they don't exist. When's the last time you saw someone order a chicken fried steak and then completely forget all about it once it was put in front of him?

Or a plate of fried chicken?

Or a fried pork chop?

Or a funnel cake?

These food items can be floating in a puddle of grease, but no one leaves them behind. They'll go ahead and eat them down to the very last soggy crumb. Not so with the hush puppy. He's shunned. Cast aside. Forgotten.

Maybe people think hush puppies are some sort of

plate decoration, you know, like parsley, or those little flowers that sometimes show up on your plate.

I (Rick) may be one of the few living people who actually pursue hush puppies. I go to certain restaurants specifically because they serve hush puppies. I've been known to get up and leave an establishment because they didn't serve hush puppies with my catfish. Bubba loves the little balls of fried dough, too.

Not getting hush puppies with catfish would be like ordering a hamburger and having them leave off the bun. It's something that should never be done. And yet, it is being done every day by narrow-thinking restaurant managers all around the country.

I am a hush puppy connoisseur. I'm not really sure what a connoisseur is, but I'm sure I'm one when it comes to hush puppies. Some people will eat a hush puppy only because it showed up on the plate. That is patronizing. I am a *true* fan of the hush puppy, and anxiously look forward to its arrival.

I'll order seconds. And thirds. I'll eat them off other people's plates. Even people I don't know. I'll order a whole plate of them. I'm more excited about the hush puppies than I am about the catfish on my plate.

That's why I have to take this opportunity to speak up for the hush puppy. Even its name implies that it can't speak up for itself. I understand this delicious fried ball of dough originally got its name because years ago, whenever someone was having a fish fry, they would take the fish and dip it into the cornmeal. Then, when the dogs came sniffing around, the cook would gather a ball of the cornmeal, drop it into hot oil, and when it was golden brown, they would give the little fried ball to the dog to get it to go away, saying, "Now, hush, puppy!"

I don't know if it's true (I haven't seen it covered on the Biography Channel yet), but it's a good story. But I guarantee that you won't read about this history of the hush puppy on any menu. No, no one gives it that much attention—or print space. And in a way, that's okay, because maybe even the hush puppy would just as soon forget its past.

♪♩♪ *"These are a few of my favorite things . . ."* ♩♪♩

So there. If you didn't know before what to put next to that big ol' pile of meat on your plate, now you do. Half a fried chicken—with a heaping cupful of . . . um, well, some kind of casserole. Both breasts of the turkey or half a pork tenderloin—*and* a pile of (say it with me, now) *d-r-e-s-s-i-n-g*. (No, not *stuffing*. Don't make me come after you!) A couple or eight catfish fillets—and about that many hush puppies.

You can eat your peanut butter and crackers for dessert.

Another tennis cake. No wonder Bubba signed up for tennis!

How We Eat:
Da Rules

By this time, it should be perfectly clear that Rick and I (Bubba) like our food. In fact, we love our food. No, scratch that. We *cherish* our food—every bite we can get.

But all the food in the world won't do a bit of good—well, maybe a *little* bit of good—if you don't observe Rick and Bubba's Rules for Eating Food Right (taken from Rick and Bubba's Rulebook of Food, which is, to date, unpublished).

Yes, ladies and gentlemen, there are some rules that govern the correct eating of the tasty morsels you raise to your lips, and if you break one, we'll find you. So, without further ado, here are "da rules."

1. *Only use one fork.* Doesn't matter how many you find at your place setting, in a restaurant or elsewhere, you just use one. Last time I ate at a hotel restaurant, there were *four* forks: three of them to the left of my plate—and I'm right-handed, thank you very much. Now, excuse us, but that's just crazy. Even we have sense enough to wipe the

gravy off our forks before attacking our cheesecake. Yes, Rick and Bubba *can* eat appetizers, salad, the main course, dessert, and anything else you care to throw at us, with just one fork.

So, please, next time you end up with four forks, just pick the one that fits you best and use it—and stick the other three in your pocket, for the pawn shop. (Hey, money's tight these days.)

Just kidding . . .

2. *Dip your soup* toward *you*. Yes, yes, we know. We've heard the old saying:

> Like little ships that sail the sea,
> I dip my soup *away* from me.

But I gotta tell ya, that sounds like a recipe for disaster— or a food fight—to me. Now, we understand that dipping one's soup away from oneself is meant to keep the soup from spill-oshing (um, don't look that word up in the dictionary; you won't find it) on your freshly starched shirt, but I'll take my chances. Last time I tried to "dip my soup away from me," I slung it right into the eye of a very testy waiter. So I practiced it at home—and propelled it across the table, at my wife, Betty, who then threatened me with bodily harm if I tried that again.

So. Lesson learned. Dip your soup, cereal, and all things wet toward your own gaping mouth. Even if it lands in your lap instead.

It's just safer.

3. *Don't make a pig of yourself at mealtime*—eat light snacks, whenever you want, instead. Yes, of course, we *all* remember being taught that we should eat three square meals a day. Well, we maintain that that's dead wrong. Of course, through the years, some doctors and diet experts (or so we hear) have amended that proposition, instead encouraging us to eat several smaller meals throughout the day. That's wrong too. You need snacks—lots of 'em—and then little meals to get you through your busy day.

Here's the logic. You get up early in the morning, and you're famished. But, hey, you don't want to eat too much for breakfast, do you? How will you work with such a

Green room snacks on the Rick and Bubba set.
A little something to keep us going.

full stomach? So instead of eating that three-egg omelet with a side of bacon (four slices) and biscuits (two), with gravy—snack a little while you're primping. Have a Pop-Tart or two, with a glass of milk (better make it whole; you can see through the fat-free stuff). Then, when you get to the table and eat your *two*-egg omelet, with a side of bacon (still four slices; you already gave up an egg), *one* biscuit, gravy, and a bowl of fruit (for health's sake), you'll have saved yourself the embarrassment of making a pig of yourself. That's especially important when the in-laws are in town. Then, when someone says to you, "Why, you didn't eat but one biscuit!" you can politely answer, "Yes, ma'am. That's 'cause I'm on Rick and Bubba's 'Hey, You Gotta Live' Diet."

And why overeat at lunch, embarrassing yourself in front of coworkers, when you can avoid it by having a granola bar here and there throughout the morning? A Snickers is even better. It's got protein. (Peanuts, you know . . .) Then when you get to McDonald's, you can order two Big Macs instead of four, and a medium fries instead of a Supersized one. (See? Smaller meal.) Think of it! You'll be saving money, saving face, and watching your waistline too!

When you get home from work, grab a package of Chips Ahoy and tear into 'em. We promise you, there'll be more at the table for the kids come suppertime. And . . . you won't make a pig of yourself. The wife won't have to throw that extra pork steak in the skillet for you. The first two will do just fine. (Look at you! Saving money again.)

And what's more enjoyable than a little cookies-and-milk treat with your family after dinner—say, *thirty* minutes after dinner—and dessert? And if you time it just right, you'll have room for a snack during *CSI*, and a bedtime snack too, so you'll sleep soundly. (Don't forget a midnight snack. It'll keep you from having to eat so many Pop-Tarts when you wake up.)

I think you get the point. Don't be a pig at the table. Instead, three average-sized meals—and little snacks, all day long.

4. *Don't use a fork when you should be eating with your hands.* If anything gnaws on me, it's watching a grown man daintily fork his Subway sandwich to death. That's just wrong. We're the grocery gurus; trust us on this one. Some foods are best eaten with your hands.

But we realize that this rule is liable to cause some confusion for those of you who have not earned your EFR certifications (that's *eating food right*, if you didn't know). So we've taken the guesswork out of the matter for you. As a public service, we would like to offer you the following detailed guidelines.

Foods Best Eaten with Your Hands

It's nothing against utensils. They come in handy when you're trying to eat pudding or pot roast. But some foods simply defy the use of a spoon or fork. Namely:

Pizza: We are not going to mince words here. We'll just come right out and say it. It bothers us when people eat pizza with a fork. *What kind of madness is this?* Don't these fork-toting folks realize that pizza is made by taking the dough in your *hands* and *tossing* it up in the air, sometimes even dropping it and having to employ the centuries-old five-second rule? That should tell us something, shouldn't it? We are not dealing with a delicate food item here. Pizza can take being manhandled.

So go on, pick up a slice and enjoy all its gooey goodness! Lick that sauce off your fingers, and then, dive in for more. You'll be following in the tradition of generations of pizza lovers before you, and you'll be setting the right example for your children and grandchildren.

But, if you simply cannot bring yourself to eat pizza with your hands, to you we say, *order something else!*

Order spaghetti.

Or ravioli.

For goodness' sake, order the eggplant!

Order anything but *pizza!*

To continue to order pizza, and then to defile it by eating it with your fork, well, it just isn't right, and we who know the proper way to eat pizza simply cannot put up with your behavior any longer.

Think about it—when they deliver pizza to your home, do they bring along plastic forks and knives? No. When they serve pizza in restaurants, do they provide forks? Well, yes, but that's only so you'll have a weapon should a duel break out over the last slice.

The bottom line is—pizza is a finger food! It has always been a finger food and it will continue to be a finger food long after we're gone. So let's not waste any more time debating what is already carved in stone ovens.

One look at a pizza tells you that it's a finger food. Why else do you think they cut it into those interesting triangle shapes? It's so the pizza slice will fit perfectly into your mouth, the size of the bite slowly increasing as you work your way down through the slice. You begin at the smallest part and then progress to the biggest, ending up with the crust, which is a totally different, but equally delicious section of the pizza—especially if it's cheese-stuffed. This is something else that we would like to address: the versatility of pizza.

Not everyone realizes this, but there are two entirely different worlds represented in the common pizza. There's the inner, cheesy part which is, of course, the *good* stuff. This is the part of the triangle that melts in your mouth and reminds you why you ordered pizza in the first place. The other part of the pizza is the crusty edge and it brings you into an entirely different world. It is, in fact, almost a different meal. It's more like eating a breadstick, and for this you will need marinara sauce. Or ranch, if you're one of those people who feel you have to be different.

Before you enter into the eating of this crusty section of the pizza, we need to tell you that there is an art to eating pizza crust. First, you will need to fold the crust at the corners, forming a sort of bun, and then you dip it into the sauce and eat it like you would a hot dog. This is one of the main reasons why you cannot use a knife and fork to cut up your pizza into bite-size pieces. If you do this, you run the risk of upsetting the delicate balance between these two worlds, and you would kill the whole pizza-eating experience.

According to the Rick and Bubba Code of Culinary Conduct, your fingers are to be your utensils for all things pizza.

Case closed.

Peel-and-Eat Shrimp: We do not understand people who eat peel-and-eat shrimp with a fork either. *Does this make* a lick of *sense to you?* Once you've got the shrimp in your hand, peeling it, why on earth would you drop it back down on your plate only to pick it back up with a fork? That's insanity, a waste of time and energy, and we don't care to discuss it any further.

Turkey Legs: There is no debating the fact that the turkey leg is a finger food. All you have to do is take one look at any old painting of a king or a Viking, and you'd know it. You won't see any of them eating a turkey leg with a knife and fork. Did Henry VIII take a fork to his turkey drumstick? No! He lifted up the turkey leg with his hand and chomped on it like a man. Did you ever think that this is why the turkey leg has a built-in handle in the first place? If it wasn't meant to be a finger food, why else would that handle be there? Sure, the turkey used it to walk, but don't get us off point here.

So, go on, lift that big ol' drumstick up to your mouth and start chewing. Only do us all a favor and save your chomping for the feasting table, like the kings and Vikings did. They didn't gnaw on it while they walked around the castle or ye ol' royal fair. They ate and licked their fingers while lying on pillows around the big feasting table, which is another point we'd like to bring up. *Why don't we do that anymore?*

Who invented the dining chair anyway?

Why can't we go back to the day when we all ate our food from a prone position? Food makes you sleepy, right? So why not already be in your napping position as you eat your meal? That way, once you finish your last bite, all you have to do is close your eyes and start your snoring. Those kings and Vikings were onto something but then some furniture designer had to come along and ruin it for all of us.

The reason we ask that you save your turkey-leg chomping for the feasting table is because it disturbs us whenever we see people walking around amusement parks, state fairs, or other such places, gnawing on a big ol' turkey drumstick. That just doesn't look right. As far as we're concerned, we don't believe turkey legs should even be sold by an outdoor vendor in the first place.

How can a royal food item like this go from a king's table to being sold out of the side of a beat-up trailer, along with sno-cones and cotton candy and who knows what else? This is a humiliating end for this regal bird. Besides, can't these vendors see that they're mixing up the whole snack food timeline?

Turkey legs and fried Snickers?

Turkey legs and funnel cakes?

Turkey legs and corn dogs?

See the problem? Maybe turkey legs are appropriate at Renaissance Fairs, but again, if you're going to eat one there, at least use your hands. And don't order the cotton candy until you're finished with the drumstick. Otherwise, you'll just look ridiculous.

Fried Chicken: We can't discuss the eating of fowl without talking about the most popular one of all—fried chicken. The problem with trying to eat fried chicken with a knife and fork is that your fork can't help but separate the meat from the crispy skin, thereby casting aside the best part of the bird. Now, members of the medical community will say that animal fat isn't healthy for us, but our take is this—if God didn't want us to eat it, then why'd he make it taste so good?

If you must use your fork and the skin does become separated from the meat, try to ignore all those medical reports and go ahead and eat it. Don't be like those people who feel so guilty that they simply push the skin to the side and eat the meat without it. What a waste! In every prominent fried chicken circle we know of, this would clearly be considered "fowl sacrilege." When eating fried chicken, health concerns should not even enter into the conversation.

"Diet" and "fried chicken" do not belong together in

the same sentence *ever*, so why pretend? Just pick up the chicken with your fingers and eat it, skin and all. Savor every tasty bite. Worry about those clogged arteries when you have to. Until then, enjoy!

Note: We also want to add that you shouldn't stress over the messiness of a fried chicken dinner. After a plate of fried chicken, you're supposed to feel like you need a bath.

Ribs: Before we talk about ribs, we need to issue a caution to all of you food lovers out there. You may already know this, but in case you don't, here is the cold hard truth: *ribs do not bring a lot of meat to the table*. In fact, I (Rick) used to not even like ribs for this very reason. I didn't think they were worth the trouble. But that was before discovering Dreamland Ribs (more on that later).

Now, if anything is a finger food, it is a rack of ribs. Ribs should *never* be eaten with a knife and fork. In some Southern states, it is against the law. We feel so strongly about this, we would like to see a mandatory rule posted in all rib restaurants:

Anyone who orders the rib platter, and then, once it arrives, makes the slightest move toward their knife and fork, will be forced to surrender the platter back to the waitstaff and will not be allowed to order ribs ever again.

We considered the death penalty for this crime, but that seemed a little harsh. But not by much.

The fun of eating a rack of ribs in the first place is getting the barbeque sauce all over your hands and face. You don't do that when you're eating the meat with a knife and fork. What would be the point of licking your fingers later if there wasn't any sauce on them?

You gotta have barbeque sauce on your fingers to make licking worthwhile.

And now that I've become a lover of ribs, I've come to realize that there is a very good reason why there isn't a lot of meat on a rib. It's so you have to chew so close to the bone that you can almost taste it. The bone adds unbelievable flavor.

If you shortcut this by carving the meat from the bone, then you're not having ribs. You're having shredded meat. It's not the same.

French Fries: For the record, we would like to see anyone who eats French fries with a fork arrested and jailed. The main reason for this reaction is because of the scene it causes. When you eat French fries with a fork, you can never stab the fries in the same place on each fry. You catch one in the middle, one at the tip, and another one about three-quarters of the way across. They end up looking ridiculous on the fork, like some kind of strange potato spider. This isn't right. Can't we leave the French fry a little dignity?

It's also hard to get ketchup on French fries when they're dangling all willy-nilly like that. You can dip the whole bunch into the ketchup, but your coverage will be spotty at best. Haven't you got better things to do with your time than to torture and embarrass French fries in this way? If you've got something against the French, find a healthier way to release it.

Burgers: Can it be true? Are there really people out there who eat their burgers with a knife and fork? We're afraid the answer is yes. We've seen them with our own eyes. Some will not only cut their burger in half, but will go a step further and cut it in half *again*. They end up with four separate sections of what was once a magnificent sandwich.

These quarters bother us because they are too close to the forbidden mini-burgers. That is why dividing a burger into quarters is considered burger abuse in many states, punishable by most of your bites not having any cheese on them. In extreme cases, you might even end up with no bottom bun on one of the quarters! Where the bottom of the bun disappears to remains a mystery.

But don't blame the bun. It's not the bun's fault. Had you taken the burger into your hands and eaten it like a man (or woman or child), every bite would have had both sides of the bun. But now, you're like that kid in the lunchroom who got carried away and made a mess out of his food, but the teacher makes him eat it anyway. Bottom bun or not, you have to eat all of your burger, and you can feel it in your gut that something isn't right. How sad.

Friends, the cheeseburger or hamburger was never meant to be quartered. Or even halved. Most buns can't hold up to that kind of pressure. We understand that successfully eating a burger, especially a double-decker, is an acquired skill. And after a few failed attempts you might be tempted to cut the burger—but resist. Stick with the whole burger, *in your hands*, and you'll eventually get the hang of it.

So, dem's da rules. Actually, there are a whole lot more in our official Rick and Bubba's Rulebook of Food, but the book got so big through the years that we could no longer bring it to the table, so we spare you.

Besides, if you'll keep the four simple rules we just gave you, you'll be eating well.

Where We Eat, Part I:

At Church

Folks, beginning in this chapter, we are going to share with you one of the best-guarded secrets to good eatin': *where* you eat is almost as critical as *what* you eat. Now, we realize that most people at most times eat at home: breakfast at the kitchen counter (or in front of the bathroom sink), dinner (or supper, if you're Southern) at the kitchen table. (Lunch doesn't count, because the majority of adults work for a living, and you can't always make a quick run home to eat that supersized combo.) But there are some awfully wonderful places to eat besides home, and if you haven't tried them, you're missing out. So in this chapter, we're going to talk to you very candidly about:

Food and Church

Most of us know that church and food go together because we have read the Bible and have seen for ourselves how many references there are to feasting. There's the account of Jesus feeding the five thousand, Jesus feeding the four thousand, and Jesus going over to his friends' and strangers' houses to eat. With all that eating going on, we can't help but come to the conclusion that Jesus loved food.

The feeding of the five thousand was the most obvious display of how much Jesus supported eating. He knew the people were hungry, and he was moved to do something about it. *That's our kind of preacher!*

But to turn one little boy's lunch of five loaves and two fishes into a feast for five thousand people was a pretty amazing miracle. Sure, we've continued trying to feed almost that many at every Southern Baptist dinner on the grounds since, but we start out with a lot more than five loaves and two fishes. But then again, they didn't have casseroles in Jesus' day.

More proof that Jesus appreciated food can be found in the passages of Scripture where he raised someone from the dead. After the miracle, he would often ask the people standing nearby to give the newly resurrected person something to eat. He knew some of them hadn't eaten for days and they needed their nourishment. If either one of us had been dead for three days and Jesus brought us back to life, we'd thank him and then ask for directions to the nearest steak house.

And what about the fact that Jesus had a Last Supper? Sure, it was the tradition of the Passover to have a meal, but Jesus could have skipped the food and had a Last Fellowship instead. Or some other event that didn't involve refreshments. But he chose to eat.

Then, after he came back from the dead himself, how did he prove to those who saw him that he wasn't a ghost? He *ate*.

And what was he doing when he met with his disciples one more time before he returned to heaven? That day he called out to them from the bank of the Sea of Galilee? He was cooking fish!

We can go on and on with more examples, but the Bible is clear that Jesus loved to eat and fellowship with his friends. So maybe that's why church and food just seem to go together. He set the standard.

And so today, you and I are the cheerful benefactors of the "church potluck." There are Baptist potlucks and

Methodist potlucks. Pentecostal feasts and Catholic feasts. A spread for the Sunday crowd, and for the Saturday crowd too. Yes, friends, the church potluck is one of the best places there is to eat.

But to get the most out of your church potluck, there is a set of never-to-be-broken rules that the eater should follow—and you *know* we can't distribute this book in good conscience without sharing them with you:

Never-to-Be-Broken Rules of the Church Potluck

1. To be considered a true potluck, there must be a ratio of at least eighteen casseroles to every meat dish.

2. The best-laid food assignments—such as saying "all those whose last names begin with the letters A–L, bring a meat dish, and all those whose last names begin with the letters M–Z, bring a dessert"—often go awry.

3. A small sampling of each food item should be set aside. Not for the servers, but for ptomaine testing later. Just in case.

4. Take a scoop of every single dish. Never allow an entrée or dessert to be left on the table untouched, unappreciated, and shunned. Somebody made that dish. Maybe they shouldn't have, but that's not important now. They did it, so the least you can do is show the food some respect, and take some of it. If it's as bad as it looks, don't worry. Refer to Rule #3.

5. Meat dishes, salads, and desserts shall each have their own table. This avoids the embarrassment of having someone's banana pudding mistaken for shepherd's pie.

6. No cutting in line. Period. This includes you, too, pastor.

7. Place saving in line is allowed, but only if the vacating person had a true emergency. In most cases, bleeding would have to be involved.

8. Do not banish desserts to another section of the room. Desserts don't deserve this kind of discriminatory treatment. Keep them in the buffet line along with all the rest of the food. If you want to give desserts their "just desserts," do it some other time.

9. If someone takes the last scoop of a dish you wanted, be the bigger man and try to be happy for him. You can always slide the scoop onto your plate when he bows his head to pray.

10. If yours is the dish that nobody sampled, don't claim it after the potluck. Pick up one of the empty dishes instead and walk proudly to your car. You can wash it and bring it back to church later.

When we pack a lunch, *we pack a lunch!*

Yes, indeed. Potlucks are one the best things this side of the pearly gates.

But wait! Did you really think that potlucks were meant just for *this* world? Oh no. The good Lord wouldn't do that to us. (Remember, "eye hath not seen, ear hath not heard . . .") You can bet your bottom dollar that there'll be potlucks up in glory too. Here's how we know.

Top Ten Reasons Why
There Will Be Potlucks in Heaven

10. Our grandmothers are there.

9. How else could you feed that many people?

8. If tofu was the only thing being served, it'd be hell.

7. To make Baptists feel comfortable with the fact that other denominations are there.

6. Some of the best cooks of all time will be there. I can't wait to try Martha Washington's biscuits. Contrary to what you may think, they are not the reason George had to get wooden teeth.

5. Many people have credited their salvation, first and foremost, to Christ's work on the cross, and in a much smaller way, to their church's covered-dish supper.

4. Because "eye hath not seen, ear hath not heard . . ."

3. God created food and he gave us freedom in him. So now we can eat for nutrition *and* we can eat just for the fun of it. It's our choice.

2. Jesus loved to eat.

1. So we can all say, "Have you had the beef stew?"

Now, sad as it is, in spite of our tribute to the casserole, some casseroles will not make it to heaven. We won't say whose won't make it—that's not for us to judge—but just know that these casseroles are one day going to be served very, very hot.

Our point is, once you and I step into that home up in the sky, we assure you, we'll have an eternity to enjoy God's great Celestial Potluck.

Until then, tell your pastor to have as many potlucks as possible right here on earth. Three times a month ought to do.

6

Where We Eat, Part II:

At the Restaurant

In times like these, we know that folks aren't eating out as much as they used to. To feed a family of four can cost a pretty penny even at the Golden Arches, if you don't make your kids eat off the dollar menu. But still, there's nothing quite as satisfying as rounding up the wife, throwing the kids in the back of your pickup, and heading out for a nice family dinner where somebody else has to do the dishes.

So in honor of the cook in all our households, we'd like to say, take a night off from cooking, honey. Let's go out!

Rick and Bubba's Favorite Places to Eat

Now, having talked you into grabbing the family and heading out to your local restaurant (hey, it's good for the economy, too, by the way; keeps folks in jobs), we'd like to share with you a list of some of the best places in the U.S. to pack your *panza* (*panza*, by the way, means "belly" in Spanish; we know this because our waiter at restaurant #9 told us so). Here they are, in no particular order.

1. Cracker Barrel

The Cracker Barrel is what life was like when you were growing up. It's your momma's cooking. Step onto its front porch, walk by the line of handmade rocking chairs, then pass through the wooden front doors of this much-loved family restaurant, and you enter your past. You're home again and life is good.

The Cracker Barrel reminds me (Rick) of my mom's cooking and all those mixed messages she used to give me. She'd cook these wonderful meals, then say, just as I'd sit down to eat: "When are you going to lose weight, Rick?"

Then, after my first plate, she'd ask, "Is that all you're going to eat?"

Not that the Cracker Barrel confronts me about my weight issues. But they do only have a double door.

Like our moms, the people at the Cracker Barrel want us to leave full. "Go ahead and eat some more" is their motto, whether it's actually posted or not. They will bring you as many biscuits and as much cornbread as you want and then they'll offer dessert, too. And if that's not enough, on your way up to the cash register, they'll try to talk you into some candy. If you're still hungry after a meal at the Cracker Barrel, it's your own fault!

In their defense, they will also encourage you to burn off some of those calories by playing that little peg game that's on each of their tables or by playing a round of checkers while sitting in the rocking chairs outside or inside in front of their fireplace. By the way, those two exercises happen to be a vital part of the Rick and Bubba exercise program.

What impresses us most about the Cracker Barrel is the simple fact that they are not embarrassed to fry a lot of what is on their menu. They make no excuses for it, nor do they try to reword the process so that it's more politically correct. They just come right out and say it right there on their menu: fried chicken, fried chicken livers, fried pork chops, fried apples, fried okra, deep-fried catfish, steak fries, chicken fried chicken, country fried steak, and country fried shrimp. And that's not even counting their Friday fish fry! They also offer grilled selections for those who want them, but they aren't forsaking the rest of us in an attempt to be cholesterol-ly correct.

Another good thing about the Cracker Barrel is that it serves breakfast any time of day you want it. They don't let the clock dictate their menu. If you want pancakes for dinner, you can have them. Scrambled eggs for lunch? You got 'em! It's breakfast all day, your way.

In our book the Cracker Barrel is long overdue for some kind of congressional award.

2. Five Guys

We happen to love the simplicity of Five Guys. If you've ever been to one of their restaurants, then you already know that their menu doesn't take a long time to read. They serve burgers, hot dogs, and fries, along with an assortment of beverages. And peanuts in the shell. There's not much else. Five Guys knows what they do well and they stick to it.

Speaking of Five Guys French fries, let's just say this—there is something about a restaurant whose motto is "A thousand fries aren't enough." Order French fries at Five

Guys and not only will they put a giant cup of fries in a bag for you, they'll dump about twice that many more on top of it.

And hey, while you're waiting for your food, why not have a fistful of peanuts? You can eat all the peanuts you want in a Five Guys restaurant. We're still trying to figure out how those two food items (burgers and peanuts) ended up together in the same restaurant. They don't really have a lot in common. But hey, the burgers are delicious, so we're not going to complain.

The Five Guys hot dog is no slouch either. It's so big you have to cut it in half to eat it. If you don't, you look like you're chomping on a log.

Five Guys—it doesn't get much better than this!

3. Hammerheads

Where else can you order a whole bucket of seafood? *A whole bucket!* We're not kidding you. You get your own little scoop of the ocean. Not only will there be all kinds of fish in there—shrimp, scallops, crab legs, even a whole lobster— but there will be appendages and tentacles hanging off the sides of the pot. Whenever I (Rick) order the seafood bucket, I feel like an otter. It's like I'm an act at Sea World and I just did good on my trick, so they brought me a treat.

4. Old Fish House

When we go to the beach in Florida, our favorite place to eat is the Old Fish House.

Before we go on, we should explain that there is the new Florida that gets trendier and trendier with each passing year. And then, there is the old Florida. The Old Fish House is old Florida at its best.

At the Old Fish House the chefs will deep-fry whatever they pull out of the ocean. I (Rick) once ate a whole crab that was fried so soft and crispy, I ate the whole thing like it was a slice of cornbread. It literally melted in my mouth. In fact, at a place like this, getting the seafood *not* fried is a special order.

5. Dreamland Ribs

Whenever we say Dreamland Ribs, it's as if we're demanding a moment of silence. In our humble opinion,

Dreamland Ribs serve the nation's best-tasting ribs. Dreamland has a pared-down menu, which means they specialize in what they specialize in—ribs. If you're hungry for ribs, then all you need to order are the ribs, extra sauce, some loaf bread, and a drink.

There was a time when I (Rick) didn't like ribs. I felt they weren't worth the trouble. But then I heard about Dreamland's ribs. Dreamland's ribs are the ribs that everyone compares other ribs to. "These are almost as good as Dreamland's," they'll say. But we say, if other ribs are only "almost as good as Dreamland's," then why not go with the best and eat Dreamland's in the first place? That's what convinced me to try them out. I did and now I'm hooked!

Believe me when I tell you, you should see the size of these ribs! I don't know where they're finding these enormous pigs, but the woolly mammoth had nothing on these guys. The ribs they serve at Dreamland are humongous! And their sauce is unbelievable! Their sauce is so good that when I get it on my face, I don't wipe it off. I just take a piece of loaf bread, swab it around my face, and then eat it.

Rick Burgess vs. barbequed ribs. Rick won.

Simply put, Dreamland's ribs are the eighth wonder of the world.

6. Kentucky Fried Chicken

We're going to get serious for a moment. We're concerned about the direction that KFC has been taking recently. It is our understanding that Kentucky *Fried* Chicken, one of our favorite restaurants, is now offering *grilled* chicken.

Did you catch that? *Grilled* chicken at a *fried* chicken restaurant. *Is that even legal?*

Ever since the introduction of this new grilled version of KFC chicken, I (Rick) have lived with the fear that one night I'm going to wake up to see the ghost of the Colonel standing at the foot of my bed, weeping.

I can't do that to the Colonel.

My favorite is the Colonel's original recipe chicken. That was the taste I first got hooked on, and that is the taste I want when I eat at KFC. I don't know what those eleven secret herbs and spices are, but combined, they create one of the best flavors on the planet.

So, don't mess with our KFC chicken!

Thankfully, they haven't changed their mashed potatoes any. They're the same as they've always been— delicious. I'm not sure how they make them (they look nothing like my mom's), but they are consistently flavorful and filling (even when you order the individual serving that, at first glance, doesn't look like it'd feed an anorexic fly).

So KFC, we say stick with the original recipe—or your

crispy fried chicken. But *grilled* chicken? Well, that may be going a little far. It might be every bit as wonderful as your original recipe, but personally, we owe the Colonel more loyalty than that.

7. Shula's Steak House

When you go into this restaurant to have a steak, take your appetite . . . and lots of cash.

Shula's steaks are so unique that you can't get them anywhere but at a Shula's Steak House. It's their own brand of aged beef, and one of their steaks will fill up your entire plate. A side doesn't have a chance next to one of their steaks. The side has to pull up on a side plate. A steak like this needs the whole plate to itself.

A friend of mine took me to Shula's after losing a friendly bet with me. I'm not a gambling man—this was more like an agreement between us. The loser of our "bet" would have to do something he might not ordinarily do. (This is how a lot of school principals end up having to shave off all their hair.)

My friend lost the contest with me, and so his penalty was to take me to the restaurant of my choice. I chose Shula's.

The food was great, as always, but when they brought the check to our table, I saw my friend's body literally flinch. I told him that I would pay him back sometime and then we'd be even. He had a better idea. He said, "Well, here's how we can be even. I'll pay this, and you pay my mortgage."

Shula's is a bit on the pricey side, but worth every penny.

8. Ruth's Chris Steak House

I love the fact that Ruth's Chris Steak House warns customers about their steaks ahead of time. When your waiter first greets you, he'll explain that your steak is going to be approximately the same temperature as the sun (the first 1,000 degrees, anyway). They warn you because they don't want you to be injured. But that's the fun of it, isn't it? Getting a steak so hot it'll brand the imprint of the fork on your tongue.

And talk about tender! Their steaks cut like you're cutting through a slice of cake. When you insert your knife, the meat just falls over in a ceremonial collapse, as if to say, "I submit."

Another great thing about Ruth's Chris Steak House

is that they don't apologize for offering real butter on your steak. They will not be dictated to by the Cholesterol Police. They know they serve a great product, and they're not above making it even better.

Paula Deen would be proud.

9. Pablo's Mexican Restaurant

The best thing about Pablo's is what happens *before* you even get seated at your table. *Free chips and salsa in the waiting area!* Now *that* is marketing! Any culture that believes a customer should be served food as soon as he or she walks through their door is all right with us.

Why don't more restaurants understand this need? Sure, other restaurants give us a beeper that lights up and vibrates when our table is ready. But as exciting as that is, we want more! We'll line up at your restaurant for up to an hour if you feed us while we're waiting.

Once at your table, Pablo's gets even better. Their food is simple, but delicious. It stands out among Mexican restaurants, which isn't easy to do. Have you noticed that most items on a Mexican restaurant menu seem to be some variation of ground or shredded beef or chicken, lettuce, cheese, tomato, and sour cream? They just keep rearranging these same items on your plate and giving it another name.

The service at Pablo's is outstanding. And they're fast. The food is brought to you before you close your menus.

Pablo's will also lift your mood. All Mexican restaurants seem to have that power. It's hard to be depressed in a Mexican restaurant. Maybe it's the music or all those big floppy hats; whatever it is, it works. Think about it—when's the last time you saw a mariachi band in group therapy?

10. Japanese Steak House

Shogun is our favorite of this type of restaurant. We love the fact that your chef comes out to perform for you. Where else do they do this? At most restaurants you barely get a glimpse of the chef—and for some restaurants, this might be a good idea.

Is there anything better than getting dinner *and* a show? Shogun gives you both. And trust us, if you've been to a

Shogun restaurant in the past and think you've seen the onion volcano, it's time to go back. They've supersized the excitement. It's no longer a simple pyramid-shaped onion on fire. Now they've got lava pouring down the side as smoke billows out the top. Some chefs even push it along like a steam train.

And if you didn't get enough butter at Shula's, you'll get even more at Shogun. As soon as they drop the meat, rice, and vegetables on the grill, they're adding butter to it all. They don't ask for a doctor's note verifying your current cholesterol level. They treat you like the adult that you are, capable of making your own food choices.

These are just some of the reasons why Shogun has made our list of favorite restaurants. And it's fun, too! Once the cooking begins, prepare yourself to start ducking because food will be flying everywhere. I can't tell you how many times we've discovered a shrimp in Sherri's purse. Days later. Sometimes weeks.

Our kids love these restaurants. As soon as they enter the doors, they get caught up in the moment and start chasing after our favorite chef, calling out, "Konetuca! Konetuca!"

Unfortunately, the chef's name is Ralph. But that's okay. He understands.

I think these restaurants are only here in America. I don't think they have them in Japan. The Japanese don't play around with their food. They just eat it. They don't need to see an onion volcano.

We, on the other hand, do. We love to be entertained in this way. And then we eat it. In that order.

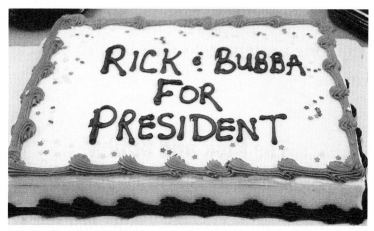

If only they had been elected! The country would have been so much better off with their Cash for Cupcakes program.

Now, unfortunately, you may not have access where you live to all of the fine restaurants in the above list. In that case, you're at the mercy of your hometown to provide you with places to dine delectably, but every one of them can become a four- or five-star restaurant, with a little help from you. Each time you eat somewhere new, rate it using the handy-dandy tool that we're about to give you. Then, if it doesn't measure up, grab a handful of big ol' signs and picket in front of the restaurant. It won't take them long to step up to the plate, so you can slide up to yours.

The Rick and Bubba Restaurant Rating System

How does a restaurant become a four- and five-star eating establishment? Some food-rating board makes the call. But who's asking us? We're the people eating at these restaurants. Shouldn't it be up to us to determine which ones get the highest ratings?

We think so. That's why we have come up with the Rick and Bubba Restaurant Rating System. Attention restaurant owners—you will need to meet the following requirements to receive high marks with our system:

- *You must provide us with a decent place to wait for our table.* If there is no place to wait, you will lose one star. It doesn't matter if you provide us with a beeper that will allow us to wander as far off as your restrooms. This is not acceptable. If we have a twenty-minute wait and your restaurant is located in a mall, let us wander the length of the mall. Is that too much to ask? We're adults. You can trust us to get back when the beeper goes off, unless there's a sale on and our wives are with us. But the men in the party will return and claim the table, so what is the harm done?

  One restaurant that provides a nice waiting room is the Aquarium. There may be a long wait, but at least they provide us with an aquarium to look at in the meantime. Some restaurants provide big-screen television sets or even a lobster tank to take a gander at. We don't care what it is, just give us something to keep our attention, and our kids' attention so they're not swinging from your ceiling fans! As entertaining as that might be for their two-year-old sibling to watch, we'd appreciate something else to focus our attention on.

- *Your name should tell us exactly what we're getting, and you should also stick with your specialty.* If you're a catfish restaurant, we should be able to assume that we're getting catfish. If you're a steak place and you have the word *steak* in your name, can we assume you're good with steak? You may have a great spinach casserole, but your specialty should be steak.

  What we don't like is when a catfish restaurant goes out of their specialty range and serves pizza. *What are y'all doing messing around with pizza?!* That's none of your business. By the same token, an Italian restaurant has no business serving nachos. It doesn't seem natural. A catfish restaurant should serve good catfish, hush puppies, and fries. It shouldn't serve egg rolls. Sure, they're all fried, but have some boundaries.

- *Restaurants that serve "mini" food items are fine, but frankly, you'll get points off if you serve the wrong kinds of "mini" items.* We are fine with mini–corn dogs, mini-burgers, and mini–breakfast sandwiches. We don't order them, but we're fine with them being on the menu. We do, though, draw the line at mini-desserts. This is an insult.

Waiters will now bring you a sliver of cake or pie and call it dessert. Do this and you'll lose a star for certain.

When I (Rick) order a chocolate soufflé, I don't want it to come out in a thimble. It's a dessert, for crying out loud! Desserts are supposed to be *big* and *fun*. They're supposed to evoke oohs and aahs as they pass by the other customers in the restaurant. That's why waiters will set some of them on fire. It's the dessert version of shock and awe. If a dessert isn't worth laying down your diet for, then why bother?

- *A seat to sit in while we order is another requirement we have for restaurants (and this is a must for us).* We are not into restaurants that make us take a tray, and then move through a line to place our dinner order. Some steak houses do this, and it's a bother. We don't want to order our meal in one place and then have to carry it someplace else to eat it.

- *Don't hand us a receipt with a place for us to write the tip on it when we haven't even been served yet!* This happens a lot at buffets. What is up with that? We're supposed to tip in faith? That's like writing a movie review before you even watch the movie, isn't it? It's not that we don't want to give the waiter a tip. We're fine with rewarding good service, even at buffets. But let us see it first.

  The bottom line is this—if you want a tip, then you need to get out from behind the register and carry our trays over to the table for us. And don't sit us so close to the lady at the next table over. Not long ago a waiter did this to me (Rick), and although the lady seemed nice enough, I think she ate half my cornbread. Which brings up our next point—

- *Give us some space between the tables!* What are you trying to do—see just how many people over the limit you can go before the fire marshal is called? Give us a little elbow room. We're tired of getting someone else's gravy on our sleeve.

- This is a biggie: *Before you remove our plates, please ask us if we're done.* Don't assume that we are finished just because our fork is resting on the side of our plate. Haven't you ever heard of eating with your hands (see previous chapter's section on this topic for help)?

  Don't ever assume that I (Rick) am done until the sopping has been completed. Don't assume my wife or my children are done either, even if all napkins are sitting in their plates. There still may be some perfectly good food there that I could eat. Leave their plates alone!

- *Don't let my glass stay empty for long.* I don't want an empty glass with only a lemon slice floating pathetically down at the bottom, in a puddle of sweet tea. Keep bringing me more ice and keep my glass full of liquid, and you'll get a star.

- *If there are kids at the table, assume that they will need tops on their beverage cups.* Don't bring out a plastic cup full of chocolate milk without the added safety of a top, because that cup *is* going to spill and you are going to be the one having to help us clean it up. This is simply a fact of life. We've faced it, and now you must too.

- *Don't be a stranger. Keep coming over and checking on us.* This is your domain. If we need something, we don't feel comfortable walking into the kitchen and finding it for ourselves. We're at your mercy.

- *Stay with your theme.* If you're a fish restaurant, be a fish restaurant. Don't go with a '50s theme that has nothing whatsoever to do with fish. Except

1950s fish, and I don't think you'd want to give the impression that your fish dates back that far.

Do the above, and you are sure to be awarded the highest honor that we can bestow on any restaurant: the Rick and Bubba Five-Star Restaurant designation! Now, *that's* something to brag about!

All right, so let's say—picketing accomplished—all of the restaurants in your hometown are stacking up to your expectations. How can you let that bright-eyed waiter or waitress know he or she has done a good job with your four-star meal? Lucky for you, we've provided you this:

Food Servers,
You'll Know We've Enjoyed the Meal When . . .

- Even though you've got an armful of dirty plates, we stop you in the aisle and hug you.
- We tip you enough to pay your kid's tuition for a semester.
- We tell you that because you were so good, we've decided to let you babysit our kids for the weekend.
- We have our picture made with you.
- We respect you so much we don't give you a nickname. (I, Rick, once nicknamed a waitress Spike. It probably wasn't a good idea.)
- We feel so sorry for you, we clear the table ourselves.
- We ask if we can video you to show other waiters how it's done.
- The next time you see us, the whole family is wearing air-brushed shirts with your name on them.
- We text you after we leave, saying something like: "Still thinking about that gr8 meal and the outstanding service! U R #1!"
- We put your performance on YouTube.
- We give you the universal sign of food appreciation. We belch.

Disrespecting the Napkin

So, now that you know the best places to eat, how to rate the ones that didn't make the cut, and how to let your servers know if their restaurants have achieved four-star status (or greater), we would like to say a few words about something that has been bothering us lately. It's this whole napkin-folding frenzy that is going on, threatening to change the world as we know it today. Do we really *need* our napkins folded into fans, stars, or animal shapes? Isn't the world going through enough change as it is?

We were getting along fine with grabbing a napkin out of a dispenser, weren't we? Sure, sometimes we couldn't get the dispenser to release the napkin without all of them coming out with it. But that shouldn't make us go to the sorts of extremes that some among us are going to now.

We're referring, of course, to the . . . well, there's just no other way to put it: the froufrouing of the napkin.

We're all for improving the napkin, if we're going to do it in ways that increase its usefulness. They can make it bigger. That seems like a good thing to do. Frankly, we don't know why they take the bib away from us after age three, anyway. Do they think we've quit spilling our food on ourselves by then? One look at our rack of ties and that'll answer that question. In fact, we're currently designing the Rick and Bubba full-body napkin. This would fit very much like a Snugglie—open in the back, with long sleeves and full frontal coverage—only it would be made out of paper.

Another thing about the napkin that disturbs us is how some waiters will seat you at your table and then immediately take your napkin and lay it across your lap. Do they really think we don't know how to operate the napkin? It's not all that difficult. Yet, they do it time and time again. We don't get it. You don't see them giving us instructions on how to use a fork. Maybe they can tell by looking at us that we are experienced fork operators. But they need to realize most of us are also equally capable of taking the napkin off the table, or out of our glass, and laying it across our laps ourselves.

Which brings us to another point—what exactly is a napkin doing in our water glass in the first place? Is this a sort of "Where's Waldo" game they're playing on us? Making us look to see where they've hidden our napkin? We're telling you, people, if we let them get away with this, the next thing we know they'll be hiding our knives and forks in the centerpiece.

To put a stop to this insanity, we suggest you rescue your napkin from your water glass immediately upon arriving at your table. In fact, rescue a bunch of them from other tables on your way to your table. Free all the napkins and save them from this humiliation. Make them have to make swans and fans out of something else. Force them to give the napkin back its dignity.

It's the right thing to do.

Where We Eat, Part III:

Other Places to Get Good Grub

Okay, so now you know that when you don't feel like cooking or have the time, good food can always be found at a local eatery. You've also learned that the church potluck is unparalleled in its ability to satisfy even the most discerning of palates. But you may not know about a couple other not-to-be-missed opportunities to scare up some delightfully mouthwatering vittles. That's what we'll tell you about next.

Many years ago, we used to have a football scoreboard show that ran down the scores of all the high school teams in our state. It was a fun show and popular with our fans, but we felt it didn't go far enough. Not only did we want to salute the great efforts of each team and their coaches, as well as their very capable school bands; we wanted to salute something else. Something that is often overlooked, but so necessary to all that is football. We wanted to start saluting the concession stands that got it right!

Yep, you heard me. We said "concession stands."

Now, of course there will always be those stands where the hot dogs still taste like the water they were boiled in, the hamburgers could be used for hockey pucks, and the candy bars are from last year's football season. We've been to 'em.

But then there are the others . . . ahh, those others . . . that make it worth the five bucks you have to pay for one hot dog. We've been to those stands, too, and from our eating experiences was born the Rick and Bubba's Concession Stand of the Week official campaign. We established rules and standards that all other concession stands had to follow to even be considered for this dubious, yet highly coveted award.

Rules for Consideration for Rick and Bubba's Concession Stand of the Week Award

The following requirements must be met for any concession stand to be honored with the Concession Stand of the Week status.

No prepackaged condiments. It can't be emphasized too much, and there is no negotiation here. Not meeting this requirement automatically disqualifies a concession stand. Mustard, ketchup, relish, and other condiments must be provided in squirt bottles or giant pumps. Packets will not be accepted because, well, quite frankly, they are from the pit of Food Hades and are not worth the effort for the amount of condiment squeezed out.

Can we hear an "Amen"?

No prefab hot dogs or hamburgers. Come on, have we really come to this, America? Have we given up *all* of our rights as consumers? Why would we want someone else deciding whether or not we want their famous sauce on our burger, or whether we want them adding other condiments, thereby messing up our delicate ketchup to mustard ratio? This is one of our most basic freedoms, and if we're not going to hold on to this, we're at risk of giving *all* our freedoms away.

We don't know about you, but we have never signed a power of attorney for our relish decisions.

So why are they rushing to judgment and making these

decisions for us? Let us make the relish call for our own hot dogs and burgers. That's a very personal call, as is the mustard and ketchup call, so never, we repeat *never*, allow anyone to pre-dress your burger or hot dog without your prior written consent. Not meeting this requirement is an automatic cause for disqualification.

Quick service. This is a must. Who wants to sit out the entire last quarter of the game waiting at the concession stand for your burger to get done?

Simplicity in the price per item. We're referring to the weird pricing game that some concession stands get into: $1.09, $0.66, etc. We don't even like the $1.50 or $1.75 prices. Let's stick with whole numbers, shall we? $1.00, $2.00, $3.00. Even in this economy, most of us would rather pay more for less hassle with the change.

Good candy selection. There is more to life than Sweet Tarts and Skittles. Let's get some chocolate in there! Is there anything wrong with that? And please, no frozen chocolate bars after they've thawed, so that you end up handing us one with that weird grayish brown look. You wouldn't serve a hot dog that had changed colors like that. Okay, maybe you would, but we don't want that sort of thing happening to our chocolate.

Chocolate is sacred.

Treat it as such.

We prefer bottled or canned sodas. If a concession stand insists on serving fountain drinks, they should make them to order. We are foursquare against a huddle of prefilled cups with already melted ice that makes the drink taste like toilet water.

The bringing in of food from established restaurants in the area is a new trend that we have seen happening in concession stands all across this great country of ours. There are pros and cons to this. If the food being brought in is kept hot and crispy (if it's originally supposed to be hot and crispy), then we're fine with this. But if it's not as good as what Walter the band parent is cooking on the grill, then why are you giving Walter the competition? If it's soggy and tastes like an old slipper, please don't be trying to pass it off on us. It doesn't do the restaurant or the customers any good.

Variety in the hot food menu. The Concession Stand of

the Week should have a wide assortment of hot foods. If you offer hamburgers and hot dogs, that's nice; but why not throw in a grilled chicken sandwich, nachos, or a gut buster (aka "Frito pie") too? Don't be tempted to add a salad, though. We realize there is substantial pressure to offer more healthy items to the public, but we believe concession stands at sports games are exempt from any new regulations concerning this. Let's face it, no one is trying to lose weight or get healthy at a sporting event or theme park. Those are "cheat days" when it comes to dieting. It might even be in the Bill of Rights.

Fresh popcorn. Now, on the subject of *popcorn*, we do have our standards. We must insist that all contenders for the Concession Stand of the Week fill the popcorn bags fresh to order. It would be good to take a cue from movie theater managers here—not on their pricing (we're not sure how they justify their prices), but on their freshness standard. Enough with those prepackaged red and white boxes that were originally filled in preparation for Y2K. The popcorn is usually stale and not nearly as good as freshly popped popcorn.

We want fresh!

We demand fresh!

Our motto: No pooped popcorn for the public! Period!

Nachos are a bold but scary endeavor. We admire concession stands that offer this amazing snack food. But the scary part is the upkeep of the cheese. We worry about this. Nacho cheese is usually purchased in a large can. Now, that right there should make you feel a little uneasy. Cheese doesn't come in cans. At least not at the grocery stores we go to. We buy our cheese in the refrigerated section. But nacho cheese is different. Apparently it's indestructible. I believe when they found Saddam Hussein hiding in his bunker, he had twelve cans of the stuff.

Another concern about this cheese is the fact that once you open the can, you've got this near vat of cheese but will most likely only use three or four cups. How do you keep the rest of it fresh, especially in a concession stand with limited space and refrigeration?

You don't! That's what we worry about, but the beauty of many concession stand workers is that they don't fret over silly little things like that. Their solution is to stick some jalapeños on it and hope no one will know the difference. If a customer does find himself with his arms wrapped around the porcelain throne all night, he'll just think it's because his team lost the ball game.

While we're on the subject, some care should be given to the freshness of the nacho chips. Who among us hasn't had to suffer through chips from two games ago, or last year's theme park anniversary? How fun was that? Concession stand operators need to realize that we don't really enjoy crunchless, tasteless, old chips with our questionably refrigerated nacho cheese. If there's no room in the cooler for the big can of nacho cheese, at least keep the chips fresh.

Keep the menu simple. Don't get into serving sausage dogs, turkey legs, portobello sandwiches, and other specialty items. Whoever came up with this ptomaine-waiting-to-happen idea of having people walk around for hours in the blazingly hot and bug-infested air, chomping on a huge turkey leg as they go (we've already discussed our feelings on this, but it doesn't hurt to go over it again) should be brought in for questioning.

Then, these turkey-leg-loving people will toss the bone onto the ground so it looks like the remains of some wild animal, causing unnecessary concern to parents of small children.

Offer corn dogs. Concession Stand of the Week contestants could also earn points by having *the much-adored corn dog* on the menu. The corn dog is a legend in its own time, and it is responsible for thousands upon thousands of smiles seen at ball games, carnivals, and theme parks everywhere. We are loyal corn dog fans, but again, give us a squirt bottle or pump of mustard and ketchup and all will be right with the world. There is nothing like making yellow and red stripes on each side of a corn dog to bring us joy.

We're simple people. But please, don't serve us frozen corn dogs. We don't want the pre-prepared kind. Stick those weenies in that incredible batter and then drop those babies into a boiling vat of grease, the way it is supposed to be done, and give them to us hot and fresh. Do that and you're a sure contender for the award!

Do not clean the grill. *Ever*. This is the last and final

tip, but it is quite possibly the most important. We also desire that the grill have cooked onions on it at all times. These onions bring a wonderful aroma and can, in some instances, neutralize the smell that sneaks out of the not-so-well-kept bathroom facilities.

With the above rules in mind, we salute you, concession stand people! For all you do to keep us fed on the ball fields and amusement parks of America, may the best among you be duly honored!

Speedy (our producer) with birthday cake
(just before the firemen arrived).

Oh yeah. Concession stands offer some fabulous fare. But even better than the all-American hot dog stand is the food fair. We've been to many; there are more we haven't tried, but since we're assuming you have no idea where to even start, we'd like to submit to you the following:

Food Fairs and Festivals of Interest

(At least they sounded interesting to us)

The Annual West Virginia Road Kill Cook-Off

Apparently, this Road Kill Cook-Off happens every year in Marlinton, West Virginia. We're not sure why, but it does. So if you've ever had a hankering for teriyaki-marinated bear, squirrel gravy over biscuits, or a dish appropriately called "The Buck Stops Here," then head to West Virginia on the last Saturday of September. You can also BYORK (bring your own roadkill) if you like.

Annual Spam Festivals

Believe it or not, there's more than one. The Waikiki Spam Jam is an annual street festival to celebrate how much Hawaiians love this great little can of meat. The festival benefits Hawaii's food bank. Hormel would be proud.

Not to be outdone in the Spam honoring race, Austin, Texas, also hosts its annual Spamarama. The festival has the Spam Ball, the Spam Cook-Off, the Spamalympics, and Spam Jam.

If you're a Spam junkie, and who isn't, then grab a can and go join in on the fun!

RC and Moon Pie Festival in Bell Buckle, Tennessee

This festival is home to the world's largest Moon Pie. We've always wanted to eat one of those (we've eaten Moon Pies, just not the world's largest!)

Each year, the folks at the festival bake a giant Moon Pie, and this monster of a cookie is then cut and served to the thousands in attendance. They even have a Festival King and Queen who do the honors of cutting the enormous Moon Pie.

The annual event is held in June, and it starts with a ten-mile run (hopefully this is optional). There are Moon Pie–themed games and competitions, and they even serve deep-fried Moon Pies. Does life get any better than this?

The Chitlin' Strut in Salley, South Carolina

Head on over to Salley, South Carolina, if you'd like to attend the annual Chitlin' Strut. We're not sure why, but the residents of Salley have proclaimed their town to be the Chitlin' Capital of the World. So far no one has challenged them for this title.

This particular food fair is held on the Saturday after Thanksgiving, and as you can probably guess, the main focus of the event is the consumption of chitlins.

The Okra Strut

Not to be outdone by the fine folks of Salley, residents of Irmo, South Carolina, have their own food festival. It's called the Okra Strut and some fifty thousand people attend the event each year. This is about the same size crowd that attends the Chitlin' Strut. In fact, a lot of food fairs draw that size of a crowd. (Has anyone ever thought that maybe it's just the same fifty thousand people going from food fair to food fair, like Trekkies, only with forks?)

A major highlight of this festival is the greatly anticipated appearance of Okra Man. (Now there's someone who got creative about finding employment in this economy. Not that being Okra Man isn't an honor that young men everywhere should aspire to.)

The World Grits Festival in St. George, South Carolina

At this festival, visitors can actually roll around in grits. If that sounds like something you've always wanted to do, you might want to check it out.

The festival runs three days, and it includes a grits-eating contest (this is different from their rolling-in-the-grits contest).

The reason that St. George hosts this festival in the first place is that back in 1985 a report came out that listed them as the town that consumed more grits per capita than any other town on the face of the earth. Believing this to be a positive thing, the town decided to have an annual festival to celebrate it.

The Hatch Chile Festival in Hatch, New Mexico

If you're from the North, South, or East you may not even know what a *chile* is. In grocery stores in our neck of the woods, *chiles* are sold under the name "Anaheim peppers." Trust us, there's a difference. (And most Tex-Mex restaurants don't have a clue what a *chile* is either. If you

Speedy demonstrates why you should take
chili label warnings seriously

ask them for a stuffed *chile*, you're likely to get a stuffed bell pepper.)

Real, honest-to-goodness *chiles*—red and green—are best found in New Mexico, and in particular, a little village named Hatch, in the southern part of the state, also known as the "Chile Capital of the World."

Each year, the Hatch Chile Festival begins with a parade, culminating in the crowning of the Chile Queen. There's also a fiddling contest, carnival rides, and a chile cook-off. Vendors all over the grounds sell everything from green chile cheeseburgers to the kind of enchiladas and burritos (with chiles) that you can only find in the Land of Enchantment.

But green chiles are not for the faint of heart. If you haven't the stomach for really hot food, make sure you go there equipped—with *lots and lots* of water.

Rick and Bubba's
Pet Peeves

All righty, then. Now that we've talked about what to eat, where to eat, and how to eat—and have even given you the *perfect* weight loss plan to meet all your dietary needs—it's time to take off the gloves and talk about our pet peeves. The first involves a little myth that is clouding the good judgment of gorgers all across our fruited plain, and that is the delusion that eating is anything but an art and an experience. Certain events across our great nation have made a mockery of the creative nature of eating. The main culprit is an affair that has called for many a barf bag, bottle of Maalox, and roll of Tums. I'm (Rick) talking specifically about "the food-eating contest."

For the love of all that is good and kind, haven't we had enough of all these food contests? Listen to us, people. We don't want to have to repeat this again—eating is *not* a contest. It is *not* a sport. It is an *experience*. And any *good* dish is a work of art.

That's our opinion, of course, but one look at us and

you'll know we know whereof we speak. We can't tell you how many times we have been asked to judge a food-eating contest. The reason for this is obvious. We are billed as the two sexiest fat men alive. We have a reputation for knowing how to eat. It is a well-deserved reputation. It is true that we do like to eat. But we have promised ourselves that we will no longer judge those "let's-see-who-can-eat-the-most" contests. We have come to the point where we have had to draw a line.

One of the main reasons for not wanting to judge food-eating contests is that these events can get pretty nasty. People often choke on the food that they're cramming into their mouths, and then someone has to be called upon to do the Heimlich maneuver on them. This, while life-saving, can get ugly. I'm not saying how far the food can shoot out when forced back into the open air, but we've seen a chunk of hot dog nearly take out a woman's eye a hundred feet away!

Another problem with food-eating contests is that the eater will often get so sick after the contest that they lose all 110 hot dogs right there in front of you. Trust us, this is not a pretty sight. One hot dog would not be a pretty sight—110 is indescribable.

And last, when you award the winner of a food-eating contest, they usually head for the restroom before you can even pin the ribbon on them. Where's the artistic merit in that?

For years we have held to the belief that eating is an art. It is an event. If you do it right, it involves sitting around the dinner table and taking the time to talk and visit with your family while you enjoy each and every beloved calorie. It's a time for the elder members of the family to teach the younger members the fine art of eating.

It was around the dinner table that my (Rick) grandfather taught me the art of bread-sopping. If you ask me, that's one of the things that's wrong with this world today. There are too many people pushing their green peas around on their plate with their fork, and failing to get a single pea to climb up onto its prongs. All they manage to do is move the peas around the plate because peas have a mind of their own.

So you can chase your peas around on your plate; where is the art or talent in that?

But thanks to my granddaddy, I now know a better way. I have seen the bread-sopping light. My grandfather showed me how to use a piece of cornbread or a dinner roll to sop up whatever was left on the plate—peas, mashed potatoes, gravy, or chunks of meat—it doesn't matter; the bread will get it all. By using bread as an edible sponge, it's easy to clear all the food off your plate and leave your fork completely out of it.

Sorry, but you can't learn things like that if you're cramming five hot dogs at a time down your throat in a food contest.

At one food-eating event, we watched a contestant dipping his hot dogs into water in order to make the buns go down more easily. That, my friends, is not a hot dog. It's weenies and soggy bread, and it's repulsive. It has ceased to be a work of art.

A hot dog needs mustard, ketchup, relish, and in certain situations, sauerkraut or chili and cheese. It does not need to be dipped in water.

While we're on the subject of hot dog fixin's, can we just sweetly remind all who serve us that we *detest* packaged condiments? It's one of our pet peeves too.

First, why do we always get that squirt of water as soon as we open the relish packet? Is this necessary? And we don't know about you, but we're still a little skittish about mayonnaise being served in a packet, especially if it's been sitting in the hot sun. Is that safe? We were both raised in fear of the two-hour-old potato salad. You don't touch a two-hour-old potato salad unless you have a death wish. But now they've come out with these sealed packets of mayonnaise that are supposed to be perfectly fine until you open them and the air gets to it. I guess that's when the clock starts ticking.

Another thing about those condiment packets that drives us crazy is the fact that when you order, say, six burgers, three hot dogs, and four orders of French fries in a drive-thru lane, why do they only give you two packets of ketchup? (Pet peeve . . .) It works the other way, too. You order one cheeseburger and a soda, and they'll toss forty-five mustard packets into your bag . . . and no napkin. Why is this? No, really . . . *why is this?!*

When it comes to condiments, we prefer the old-fashioned pumps. In fact, if you ever want us to come to your town and judge a food *cook-off* (remember, we don't do contests), do *not* serve the condiments in packets. Otherwise we'll be forced to boycott your event. We want pumps! This subject is not up for debate. In fact, it's a rider in all of our contracts. Pump condiments or no Rick and Bubba. It's just another line we had to draw in our careers.

And here's another pet peeve. Whenever I (Bubba) go to a fast-food restaurant, I can never get my hands on the salt. Yes, I understand why most of these establishments are no longer putting the salt and pepper shakers on the tables. In our country's current economic state, anything not nailed down is fair game . . . for the pawn shop. But for cryin' in a bucket! Why can't they at least put those little paper packets within reach? Last time I went to get a fast-food burger, someone had conveniently forgotten to salt the meat. So I reach for the salt shaker. Predictably, it's not there. So I go up to the condiment area, where you can—believe it or not—*pump* your ketchup and refill your soft drinks—but cannot find the salt packets. That's because, like the shakers, *they're not there*!

So, undeterred, I head to the counter—which is swarming, at all three cash registers, with people. I couldn't approach a cashier if I wanted to. So I yell—very politely, mind you—"Hey, could I get a couple of packets of salt?" at which point the entire group of fifty or so other customers turns around and bores holes through me. I even hear one of them mutter, "Hey buddy, wait yer turn."

So I get in line and wait until all sixteen and a half *other* customers in that line place their orders, wait until the frycook kid finishes frying the French fries that weren't ready when the swarm of customers came through the door, and *then* wait until said customers get their sacks of grub.

By this time I'm chewing on the inside of my cheek. I turn and look at the woman in the line next to me. Maybe it was the smoke coming out of my ears, I don't know, but she says, "You look frustrated."

Ya *think*?

Finally, I'm standing face-to-face with an already-frazzled cashier, and fearful that I might say something

I shouldn't—hey, I'm human too—I simply mutter, "Salt, please." And with a huff, she reaches under the counter and retrieves a *single* packet of salt. From the look on her face, I know better than to ask for more.

Folks, it is our sincere hope that you never have to deal with any of these pet peeves of ours. Food is good, anytime, but life is so much easier when things go your way.

9

Rick and Bubba's
Grocery Store Chain

Since our wives have often referred to the grocery store as our second home, we have decided to capitalize on this fact and are looking into the possibility of having our own chain of Rick and Bubba grocery stores.

We can hear your applause now.

So what would an R & B grocery store look like? Well, here are just a few of the features that we have listed in our business plan:

- Our store's clerks would be forbidden to ask whether you want paper or plastic bags. Who needs that kind of pressure after an hour of shopping? You've already had to make hundreds of decisions throughout the store.

    Do I want regular Oreos or the ones with mint-flavored filling?

    Do I want white bread, wheat bread, or monkey bread?

Do I want the quart of cookie dough ice cream or the fifty-gallon drum?

Decisions, decisions, decisions. By the time you finally steer your cart up to the counter, you don't want to have to answer yet another question. Our checkout clerks will be directed to keep their paper or plastic inquiries to themselves. But rest assured, they won't simply drop your items back in your cart like some of those warehouse stores do, either.

You don't need your groceries rolling all over the back of your car, making it sound like you've just busted a head gasket. No, at our stores, your groceries will be placed in those wonderful old grocery bags of days gone by, the ones that were already double-strength (no double-bagging necessary), with sturdy handles for easy carrying. Remember those? They were great, weren't they? Someone came along and made stores get rid of them for the "environment," but what have all these plastic bags done for the environment? And that's not even counting all the times they've busted on the way out to the parking lot. What's spilled pickle juice on hot asphalt doing to the environment? Has anyone studied that?

- We love the idea of the kiddie seat on shopping carts, but we say why stop there? Why not have carts with a mommy or daddy seat, too? In fact, why not let the kids push their parents around the store for a change? We're the ones paying for everything, right? Why shouldn't we be the ones getting pampered? If we had a seat to sit on, we'd be inclined to shop a lot longer, and store profits would increase. A mommy or daddy seat makes economic sense at a time in our world when little else does.

- No weird fruit would be sold at our stores. If it's not an easily recognizable fruit (banana, apple, orange, or even kiwi . . . okay, maybe not kiwi), it will not find a home in our stores.

     Sorry, horned melon. We're not ready for

horns or fuzz or other weirdness on our produce. We might never be.

Our apologies, UFO peach (its real name).

Regrets, all you other strange-looking fruits and vegetables that have somehow found your way into our grocery stores. (Like square watermelons. We still want our watermelons oval shaped.) In the Rick and Bubba grocery store chain, we will have none of this. Only apples, oranges, bananas, and melons the way apples, oranges, bananas, and melons used to be.

- We don't like all these "buy one, get one free" deals. I (Rick) don't want to have to buy a giant bottle of mustard in order to get another giant bottle of mustard free. My family doesn't go through that much mustard. My county doesn't go through that much mustard. All I want is a little jar of mustard and I'm good to go. But store managers tempt us with these "buy one, get one free" deals, and we fall for them. Before we know it, our shopping cart looks like we're buying groceries for the entire Southern division of Little League. This is why our chain of grocery stores won't offer any "buy one, get one free" deals.

- Thanks to the Bun/Hot Dog Treaty of 2010 that we successfully negotiated, the weenies and the hot dog buns in our stores will have coordinated packaging.

- For years we have wondered why candy and health food are found in the same grocery aisle. What kind of sick, twisted mind came up with that arrangement? Why would you put every kind of chocolate known to man on the same aisle as rice milk? Does this make sense to anyone? It doesn't to us, and it will never happen in our grocery stores.

As a matter of fact, we won't have any health food at all. If you want healthy food, go to a gym snack bar. People go to the grocery store to get real food. We're not going to have any zero-fat potato chips. If you want to eat potato chips, then eat potato chips. If you don't want to eat potato chips, then don't eat potato chips. But we're not going to cater to those tampering with our junk food. The reason this country is going to you-know-where in a handbasket is we started letting people mess with our junk food. We don't need a healthy donut. It's a donut, people! It's not supposed to be healthy!

- When holidays come, we'll make extra sure that our stores carry the same wonderful products that you're seeing in all of the newspaper inserts and magazines. If there's anything that ticks me off, it's when I get a newspaper insert showing me something like, say, pumpkin spice coffee creamer, and then when I get to the grocery store—any grocery store—it's nowhere to be found. One time I (Bubba) got the Sunday paper during the Christmas season, and there were ads galore for all of the seasonal coffee creamers: gingerbread, peppermint chocolate, you know. The good, Christmasy stuff. But was there a grocer within twenty miles that had it? Noooo. This scenario will *not* take place in Rick and Bubba's grocery store chain.

- Coupons will not be allowed in our stores. We understand the need for savings, especially in this uncertain economy. But let's be honest. Who wants to get stuck behind some lady going through her coupons and arguing with the clerk about whether or not they're outdated?

    Once I (Rick) was stuck in a line behind a woman who was doing just that. I finally asked the clerk, "Look, how much are the savings?"

    He said, "Forty-one cents."

    I said, "Here."

    Then I handed the clerk two quarters just to get her out of the line.

- Another change that we plan on making in our stores is this: we are going to put an end to all the confusion in the toilet paper aisle. We never have understood this. There are jumbo rolls, regular rolls, mini rolls, and wet wipes. Can't there be some consistency here? Most of us don't want a roll of toilet paper that's as big as a sewer drain. We don't want to have to figure out which has more paper—twelve regular rolls or six jumbo rolls. Just give us four rolls of toilet paper the way stores used to. And don't make them so big they can't fit on the spinner. We want toilet paper, not pillows. Has anyone written to these companies to inform them of this problem?

Someone should let them know that we don't need lotion on our toilet paper either. Whose bright idea was that? Get real. Nix the lotion.

And our stores won't sell any recycled toilet paper either. Some things were not meant to be recycled!

- Forget all the choices you have in toothpaste now. You won't get that at our stores. But that's okay, because toothpaste has gotten ridiculous. We're knocking plaque off, smelling like watermelon and blueberries, whitening our teeth so that they could burn through the retina of oncoming pedestrians. Who needs all of this craziness?

We propose to offer only three types of toothpaste in our stores—Colgate, Crest, and maybe one off-brand for all you rebels out there. And that's it. Too many choices have us loitering in the toothpaste aisle for far too long.

Stores, in general, offer way too many choices and are way too big these days. They're overwhelming. We have super-everything. Super Targets, Super Kmarts, Super Wal-Marts, and that's not even counting all the discount stores, like Sam's Club and Costco. The average grocery store today is the size of a couple of football stadiums. Whatever happened to the mom-and-pop stores? I'll tell you what happened—they visited one of the mega-stores to check up on their competition and got lost. They never found their way back out.

Our stores are going to be small and intimate, with just three choices of toothpaste. And maybe one brand of mouthwash . . . but we're still thinking about it.

- Ice will not be up by the checkout counter at our stores. We have never understood this practice. Why is ice on the honor system? They wouldn't put a bunch of chickens on a rack by the front door and let everyone just walk by and take what they need.

  Don't you feel stupid paying for ice anyway? I (Rick) always do. Like the seventeen-year-old behind the register is thinking what kind of loser I am to be plunking down $1.50 for a bag of ice that I could have made at home myself had I just thought ahead.

- Dog food would come in easier-to-handle sizes in our stores. Are dog food companies in some kind of contest to see who can make the biggest bag of dog food? This is getting out of hand. When you have to ask to borrow the forklift just to get a bag of dog food up to the checkout counter, something is wrong. Dog food should not have to be strapped down to the top of your car, and if you do have to strap it down, it shouldn't create a sunroof.

- We will have clear and easy-to-follow signage in our grocery stores that lets you know exactly what is down each aisle. Shopping in one of our stores will not make you feel like you're in an episode of *Lost*. Our signs may be a little different from what you'd expect. For instance, we'll have signs that give you the "feel" of the aisle. Signs like: "This aisle is fun, but some of the items here aren't so good for you." Then, there will be signs that say: "Not so much fun down here, but every-thing's good for you." And of course, the ones that are a blend of both—the "sort of fun, sort of good for you" aisle.

- Soft drinks will not have their own aisle in our stores. They don't need an entire aisle. Grocers only started giving them a full aisle when soda companies started froufrou-ing their drinks, and needed more room for all the new flavors. But we say, do we really need Fizzy Apple–flavored soft drinks? Or Cranberry Crème? If you want froufrou drinks, go to Starbucks.

- And forget reading the label on products. We never have agreed with this new packaging requirement, so we're not going to insist on it at our stores. We'll just carry the product and you don't ask too many questions. If you're like us, you'll appreciate this. Who wants to have to read labels in the grocery store? We know we don't. We don't want to have to be Agent 007 in the grocery store. When we go shopping, our motto is "Surprise us." If yours is, too, you'll love our stores.

Rick and Bubba's
Secret Recipe File

We couldn't close this book without offering our readers some of the "best of the best" recipes we know of, and more than just the ones we've sprinkled here and there throughout the book. These recipes are fresh from the vault, and we hope you enjoy them.

Rick and Bubba's Almost Nearly Perfect Bar-B-Q Sauce

Combine Worcestershire sauce, vinegar, meat-flavored spaghetti sauce, sugar, and catsup (Heinz only) to taste, and mix well. (Don't ask us how much of each to use! We just keep adding and stirring until we like it!)

Bubba's World-Famous
Homemade Macaroni and Cheese

(Okay, it's his mom's recipe. Bubba can't cook,
but he wanted to be included.)

An inexpensive but "Bubba"-licious dish that is a
perfect meal for all of you newlyweds, singles,
seniors, and overtaxed middle class.

Ingredients:

1½ cups elbow macaroni	½ teaspoon salt
3 tablespoons butter	Dash of pepper
3 tablespoons all-purpose flour	¼ cup minced onion (optional)
2 cups milk	2 cups shredded sharp processed cheese

Directions:

- Preheat the oven to 350 degrees. Cook the macaroni in boiling salted water until tender. Drain.

- In a separate pan, melt butter, blend in flour, add milk, and cook, stirring constantly until thick.

- Add salt, pepper, onion, and cheese. Stir until cheese is melted.

- Mix the sauce with the macaroni, and pour into a 1½-quart casserole.

- Bake for about 45 minutes or until the top is golden brown and bubbly.

Sherri's Famous Chocolate Sauce

Ingredients:

1/2	cup cocoa
3/4	cup sugar
2/3	cup evaporated milk
1/3	cup light corn syrup
1/3	cup butter
1	teaspoon vanilla

Directions:

- Combine the cocoa and the sugar in a medium saucepan; then blend in the milk and the corn syrup.

- Cook over medium heat, stirring constantly until the mixture begins to boil.

- Boil and stir for 2 to 3 minutes more; then remove from heat.

- Stir in the butter and vanilla.

- Serve warm over Rick and Bubba's Buttermilk Biscuits (recipe follows), to make "Sherri's Famous Chocolate Biscuits" (we have these every Christmas morning). This sauce is also great over pound cake and ice cream!

Rick and Bubba's Buttermilk Biscuits

Ingredients:

1	cup sifted flour
1/2	teaspoon salt
2	teaspoons baking powder
1/8	teaspoon baking soda
1/8	cup shortening
1/2	cup milk
1	teaspoon lemon juice or vinegar

Directions:

- Preheat the oven to 450 degrees.

- Sift the flour, salt, baking powder, and baking soda together.

- Cut in the shortening. Set aside.

- In a small bowl, combine the milk and lemon juice or vinegar. Stir into the flour mixture to make a soft dough.

- Turn the dough onto a floured surface, and knead until soft and elastic.

- Roll the dough into a rectangle, about 1/2 inch thick, and then cut into biscuits.

- Place the biscuits on an ungreased cookie sheet and bake for 8 to 10 minutes.

Rick's Momma's Famous Fudge

(I always volunteered my mom to make fudge
for all class parties. It's why I passed.)

Ingredients:

3 cups sugar	1 tablespoon butter
1/3 cup cocoa	1 teaspoon vanilla
Dash of salt	2–3 tablespoons peanut butter
1 1/2 cups milk	

Directions:

- In a medium saucepan, combine the sugar, cocoa, and salt. Add the milk.

- Heat and stir over medium heat until mixture comes to a boil.

- Continue cooking until the mixture reaches soft ball stage on a candy thermometer. Test its doneness by dropping a spoonful of fudge into cold water. (This is usually around 20 minutes after it first comes to a boil.)

- Remove from heat and add the butter and vanilla. Let cool to lukewarm temperature.

- Add the peanut butter. Beat the mixture until the fudge begins to thicken.

- Pour on a buttered plate or platter. Wait until the fudge has formed and then . . . enjoy!

Burgess Farm Cheesy Squash Casserole

Ingredients:

1   pound Burgess Farm summer (crookneck) squash, chopped
    (I guess you can use your own, if you have to.)
1   small onion, chopped
2   tablespoons butter
2   eggs, beaten
1   cup milk
1   cup grated American cheese
1   cup cracker crumbs
    Salt and pepper

Directions:

- Preheat the oven to 375 degrees.

- Combine the squash, onion, and butter. Cook the squash until both the onion and the squash are tender; drain and mash.

- Add the remaining ingredients, and then pour the mixture into a buttered casserole dish.

- Bake until lightly browned.

Rick and Sherri's
"No One Gave Me a Bailout" Rice-a-Beanie

Here is a tasty (and cheap) recipe that Sherri and I lived off of when we were barely getting by. From the looks of the economy, it might be time to drag it out again.

Ingredients:

1   box Rice-a-Roni, the San Francisco treat (to be prepared according to the directions on the box)

1   pound cheap ground beef, browned (hopefully it's not brown until *after* you've cooked it)

1   can pinto beans

Directions:

- When the water starts boiling for the rice, add the box of Rice-a-Roni and cook.

- Add the cooked ground beef and pinto beans.

- Turn the heat to low and cover.

- Cook until the beans are hot.

Rick and Bubba's World-Famous "Goat Drop Cookies"

(Makes about 4 dozen cookies.)

Ingredients:

- 2 cups sugar
- 1/2 cup evaporated milk
- 2 tablespoons cocoa
- 1 stick butter
- 1 teaspoon vanilla extract
- 2 1/2 cups quick-cooking oats

Directions:

- Combine the sugar, milk, cocoa, and butter in a medium saucepan.
- Bring to a boil over medium heat, stirring constantly. Boil for 1 minute.
- Remove from heat; stir in the vanilla.
- Add the oats and stir to blend thoroughly.
- Drop by teaspoonfuls onto waxed paper.

Rick's Cheap Solution for the Guy Who Has a TV, a Bed on the Floor, and an Old Couch*

Ingredients:

½ pound ground beef

Hamburger buns that are on sale (but with nothing fuzzy growing on them yet)

Your favorite barbeque sauce (or ours—see recipe on page 181)

Directions:

- Preheat the oven to 350 degrees.

- Brown the meat in a skillet (if you don't have one, borrow one from a girl).

- Drain the meat (you might need to borrow a strainer too).

- Start toasting the buns in the oven (directly on the rack, if you don't have a baking sheet).

- Pour the meat out of the strainer and back into the skillet.

- Add the barbeque sauce while stirring the meat.

- Take the hamburger buns from the oven.

- Scoop out a serving of sauce-covered meat.

- Place on the buns and eat.

---

* This sounds similar to a Sloppy Joe, but mine is sloppier and my name's not Joe.

Rick's Momma's World-Famous Cornbread

Ingredients:

1	cup yellow cornmeal
1	cup flour
1/2	cup sugar
4	teaspoons baking powder
1/2	teaspoon salt
1	egg, beaten
1	cup milk
1/2	cup cooking oil

Directions:

- Preheat the oven to 425 degrees.

- Mix all ingredients until well blended.

- Pour into a greased 8-inch square pan. (No, make that an iron skillet or my mother will be furious.)

- Bake for 20 minutes or until light golden color. A knife inserted in the center should come out clean.

Rick's Perfect Grilled Pork Tenderloin

(This is one of those foods that make you
glad to be a Gentile.)

Ingredients:

Pork tenderloin
Brown sugar

Directions:

- Heat the grill wide open for about 15 minutes.

- Take the pork tenderloin and turn off one side of the grill. (If
  using charcoal, only heat one side of the grill.) Don't put the
  tenderloin on the side with direct heat.

- As the tenderloin cooks, take some brown sugar and sprinkle
  on top of the tenderloin and watch it melt into a caramel that
  bathes the tenderloin. Continue to add the brown sugar every
  time it melts, until meat is well coated.

- Cook, covering between additions of brown sugar for 45
  minutes to an hour, until done, checking occasionally.

Sherri's Delicious Salmon and Pasta

(A classic at the Burgess household)

Ingredients:

Salmon
Olive oil
Salt and pepper
Pasta
Pesto sauce

Directions:

- Purchase some fresh salmon from your favorite grocery store, and wash it. (It's important to cook the salmon the same day you buy it.)

- Preheat the oven to 350 degrees.

- Rub the salmon with olive oil, and sprinkle with salt and pepper.

- Place in a baking dish and bake for about 20 minutes. (Keep checking to make sure the fish doesn't overcook.)

- Boil some pasta, drain, and then pour the pesto onto the pasta and mix gently.

- Serve pasta alongside cuts of salmon. Add a nice, fresh salad and enjoy!

Greg Burgess Bread Lovers' Easy Drop Rolls

Ingredients:

1½ sticks butter
1   package dry yeast
2   cups warm water
¼   cup sugar
1   egg, slightly beaten
4   cups self-rising flour

Directions:

- Melt the butter and let it cool. Dissolve yeast in warm water.

- Add the remaining ingredients and stir until well blended. (Dough will be sticky.)

- Place in an airtight covered container and store in the refrigerator for several hours before using.

- *To serve*, preheat the oven to 400 degrees. Spoon the dough into greased muffin tins and bake for 20 minutes. (The dough can be kept a week in the refrigerator.)

Betty's World-Class Chicken Tetrazzini

Ingredients:

1	(16-ounce) package vermicelli
1/2	cup chicken broth
4	cups cooked, chopped chicken
1	can cream of mushroom soup
1	can cream of chicken soup
1	can cream of celery soup
1	(8-ounce) container sour cream
1	(6-ounce) jar or can of mushrooms (optional)
1/2	cup shredded Parmesan cheese
1	teaspoon pepper
1/2	teaspoon salt
2	cups shredded cheddar cheese

Directions:

- Preheat the oven to 350 degrees.

- Prepare the vermicelli according to the package directions; drain. Return to the pot and toss with the chicken broth. Set aside.

- In a very large bowl, stir together the chopped cooked chicken and the next 8 ingredients. Add the vermicelli and toss well. Spoon the mixture into two lightly greased (I use Pam) 13x9-inch baking dishes. Sprinkle evenly with cheddar cheese.
- Bake, covered, for 30 minutes. Uncover and bake about 5 minutes more or until the cheese is bubbly.
- Note: This also freezes well. To use, thaw overnight in the refrigerator. Let stand for 30 minutes at room temperature, and bake as directed.

Lasagna by Betty

Ingredients:

1–2 pounds ground chuck
1 large jar spaghetti sauce (20—32 ounces)
1½ cups water
   Canned or fresh mushrooms (optional)
   Dried or fresh oregano
3 cups shredded mozzarella cheese, divided
1 cup shredded Parmesan cheese, divided
2 eggs
1 (15-ounce) tub ricotta cheese
   Dried or fresh parsley
   Salt and pepper to taste
1 package lasagna noodles (no-boil kind)

Directions:

- Preheat the oven to 350 degrees.

- Brown the ground chuck in a large skillet. Add the spaghetti sauce and the water. Add mushrooms if you like and oregano. Simmer for 30 minutes.

- Meanwhile, in a large bowl, mix 2 cups of the mozzarella cheese, 1/2 cup of the Parmesan, the eggs, the ricotta cheese, the parsley, and the salt and pepper.

- In a lightly greased 13x9-inch pan, pour 1 cup of the sauce mixture. Place a layer of the noodles on top of the sauce, and pour in another cup of sauce. Next, spoon half of the cheese mixture on top of the sauce. Continue layering as follows: noodles, sauce, cheese, noodles, sauce, etc. On top of the last layer, sprinkle the remaining Parmesan cheese. Cover with foil and bake for 45 minutes. Remove the foil and sprinkle the remaining mozzarella on top. Bake for an additional 10 minutes.

Hush Puppies by Rick

Ingredients:

1½   cups white cornmeal
4   teaspoons flour
2   teaspoons baking powder
   Salt to taste
1   tablespoon sugar
¼   cup minced onion
1   egg, slightly beaten
1   cup boiling water
   Vegetable oil to cover while frying

Directions:

- In a large mixing bowl, combine the cornmeal, flour, baking powder, salt, sugar, onion, and egg. Blend well. Add the water rapidly while stirring. (The water must still be boiling when adding.) Set the bowl aside.

- In a Dutch oven or fry pot, heat the oil to 370 degrees. Drop the cornmeal mixture by rounded spoonfuls into the hot oil. Cook until golden brown. Drain on paper towels.

- Makes about 36 hush puppies.

We have *lots* more recipes that will soon be featured in our brand-new Rick and Bubba cooking magazine. Watch for it! But for now, we leave you with these five simple words that have become our motto: *eat, drink, and be full!*

Another birthday cake delivered to the Rick and Bubba studios.
(We alone are keeping five Birmingham bakeries in business.)

Appendix

Rick and Bubba's Grub Definitions

All You Can Eat: This term is very misleading. We were asked to leave an "all you can eat" Chinese restaurant once because our "all you can eat" was "more than they wanted to serve." They said, "You eat too much! You leave now!"

Barbeque: This term has come to mean a lot of things over the years, but basically it means several men standing around a grill, discussing various ways to solve their favorite football team's problems (even though most of these men have never played or coached the sport). There's something about an outdoor grill that turns all of us men into football geniuses.

Fast Food: We understand this phrase, and we're sure you do too. But many fast-food restaurant workers can't seem to grasp the concept. What's so misleading about the term "fast food" is the word *fast*. Many fast-food restaurants are not all that fast. We believe they should change their title from "fast-food restaurants" to "'Pull forward and we'll bring your order out to you when it's ready' parking lots."

Fish Fry: This means "a yard full of family members gossiping and complaining about each other over fish, fries, and hush puppies." The term also denotes a sense of danger, due to the fact that some of these relatives are usually standing close to boiling-hot grease.

Formal Dining: Anywhere that requires shirt and shoes. And probably a fork.

"Gimme just a bite": This is a phrase that sounds better than *"I want to slobber on your food so you will be horrified enough to just give me the whole plate."* Wives will often use this ploy on their husbands, and vice versa. Saying, "Gimme just a bite" to strangers sitting at nearby tables in restaurants, however, is frowned upon by most civilized people.

Meat and Potatoes: This is an almost forgotten phrase, but basically, it means "real food," not like the kind they serve in froufrou restaurants where they give you very little food but all-you-can-eat pâté (which is French for "glob of pureed liver"). With a meat-and-potatoes meal, your plate will be fully loaded, without a lump of pâté in sight!

Midnight Snack: The word *midnight* is relative. When we grab a snack, we call it a "midnight snack" because it must be midnight *somewhere*.

Potluck: This word literally means "a table full of bowls and platters of food that one plays a sort of Russian roulette with" (hence the "luck" part). When eating at a potluck, you have no idea which dishes were made by people who *can* cook, and which ones were made by people who *think* they can cook. It is important to know the difference, and you won't know this until you've been attending the church or group for at least a year. Or signed up for their newsletter, where hospital reports and prayer requests are listed.

Acknowledgments

Rick and Bubba would like to thank first and foremost, *Jesus Christ*. Without you, we as a human race have no hope. Thank you for providing the sacrifice that we could never provide for ourselves.

And thanks to:

Martha Bolton . . . even though she is skinny, she can eat with the best of 'em.

All the great folks at Thomas Nelson

David Sanford

Cox Broadcasting

Syndicated Solutions

Calvin "Speedy" Wilburn

The Real Greg Burgess

Michael Helms

And the greatest, most powerful, best-looking listening audience in the world! You ladies and gentlemen make it all happen. Without you, no one cares!

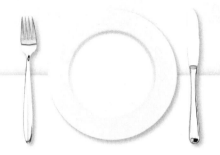

Rick and Bubba's
Recipe Index

Itty-Bitty

If you liked this book, check out *these*

Rick & Bubba

masterpieces

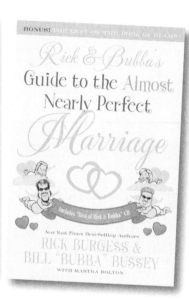

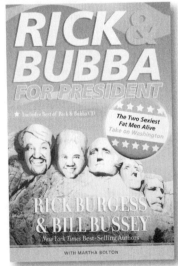

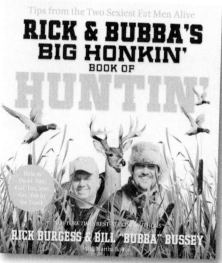